PRAISE FOR

The Soloist

"Steve Lopez's book about Nathaniel Anthony Ayers, a black musician and paranoid schizophrenic, makes you want to dust off your dreams and scrub the world clean." —*Pittsburgh Post-Gazette*

"The next time one of my college students asks me why I chose journalism as a profession and writing about music and musicians as a specialty, I will respond with two names: Nathaniel Ayers and Steve Lopez." —*The Irish Echo*

"The book is a sign that good people still walk among us. The outpouring of support from people of all walks of life made me want to be a better person." —*Minneapolis Star Tribune*

"*The Soloist* directly recounts the unusual, ultimately heartwarming tale, but not before the author takes readers on a harrowing journey through the tougher elements of both mental-health treatment and the lower depths of downtown L.A. . . . Lopez's writing is as propulsive as good fiction . . . inspirational." —*BookPage*

"Powerful." —*Los Angeles Magazine*

"An unforgettable tale of hope, heart and humanity." —*Parade*

"By turns harrowing, winsome and inspiring . . . A deeply moving story." —*Library Journal* (starred review)

"[A] compelling, emotionally charged tale of raw talent and renewed hope." —*Booklist* (starred review)

continued . . .

"With self-effacing humor, fast-paced yet elegant prose and unsparing honesty, Lopez tells an inspiring story of heartbreak and hope."

—*Publishers Weekly* (starred review)

"Lopez brings empathy, intelligence and humor to his poignant portrait. . . . Energetic prose delivers powerful insights on homelessness and mental illness."
—*Kirkus Reviews*

"Written with elegant spareness, there are no punches pulled in this portrait of Nathaniel Ayers, but, God, do you root and hope and pray for him. Many books claim to be about redemption and the affirmation of the human spirit, but they are false gospels. *The Soloist* is singularly and unforgettably true in all respects."

—Buzz Bissinger, author of *Friday Night Lights*

"Steve Lopez is a terrific reporter. *The Soloist* is poignant, wise and funny."
—Sylvia Nasar, author of *A Beautiful Mind*

"*The Soloist* is a symphony, providing an honest look at mental illness, human dignity and the need for social connection. It is also a call to action. As masters of their arts, Steve Lopez and Nathaniel Ayers deserve a standing ovation."   —Michael J. Fitzpatrick, Executive Director, National Alliance on Mental Illness (NAMI)

"Steve Lopez puts a face on mental illness and in doing so, shows us how friendship can alter the lives of both the disenfranchised and those who reach out to them. *The Soloist* is a poignant reminder that no life is insignificant. An utterly compelling tale."

—Pete Earley, author of *Crazy: A Father's Search Through America's Mental Health Madness*

The Soloist

A Lost Dream, an Unlikely Friendship, and the Redemptive Power of Music

Steve Lopez

BERKLEY BOOKS, NEW YORK

THE BERKLEY PUBLISHING GROUP
Published by the Penguin Group
Penguin Group (USA) Inc.
375 Hudson Street, New York, New York 10014, USA
Penguin Group (Canada), 90 Eglinton Avenue East, Suite 700, Toronto, Ontario M4P 2Y3, Canada
(a division of Pearson Penguin Canada Inc.)
Penguin Books Ltd., 80 Strand, London WC2R 0RL, England
Penguin Group Ireland, 25 St. Stephen's Green, Dublin 2, Ireland (a division of Penguin Books Ltd.)
Penguin Group (Australia), 250 Camberwell Road, Camberwell, Victoria 3124, Australia
(a division of Pearson Australia Group Pty. Ltd.)
Penguin Books India Pvt. Ltd., 11 Community Centre, Panchsheel Park, New Delhi–110 017, India
Penguin Group (NZ), 67 Apollo Drive, Rosedale, North Shore 0632, New Zealand
(a division of Pearson New Zealand Ltd.)
Penguin Books (South Africa) (Pty.) Ltd., 24 Sturdee Avenue, Rosebank, Johannesburg 2196, South Africa

Penguin Books Ltd., Registered Offices: 80 Strand, London WC2R 0RL, England

While the author has made every effort to provide accurate telephone numbers and Internet addresses at the time of publication, neither the publisher nor the author assumes any responsibility for errors, or for changes that occur after publication. Further, publisher does not have any control over and does not assume any responsibility for author or third-party websites or their content.

The author has set aside a portion of all advance payments and royalties for the support and benefit of Nathaniel Ayers.

PRINTING HISTORY
G. P. Putnam's Sons hardcover edition / April 2008
Berkley movie tie-in trade paperback edition / October 2008
Berkley trade paperback edition / May 2010

Berkley trade paperback ISBN: 978-0-425-23836-3

The Library of Congress has cataloged the G. P. Putnam's Sons hardcover edition as follows:

Lopez, Steve.
   The soloist: a lost dream, an unlikely friendship, and the redemptive power of music / Steve Lopez.
      p.   cm.
   ISBN 978-0-399-15506-2
   1. Ayers, Nathaniel Anthony.   2. Violinists—United States—California—
   Biography.   3. Homeless persons—California—Los Angeles.   4. Skid row—
   California—Los Angeles.   I. Title.
   ML418.A96L66   2008   2007046314
   787.2092—dc22 [B]

PRINTED IN THE UNITED STATES OF AMERICA

20   19   18   17

PUBLISHER'S NOTE: This book describes the real experiences of real people. The author may have disguised the identities of some, and in some instances created composite characters, but none of these changes has affected the truthfulness and accuracy of his story.

For Alison and Caroline,
who made Nathaniel part of our extended family.
And for Nathaniel's mother, the late Floria Boone,
whose love never wavered.

I'm on foot in downtown Los Angeles, hustling back to the office with another deadline looming. That's when I see him. He's dressed in rags on a busy downtown street corner, playing Beethoven on a battered violin that looks like it's been pulled from a Dumpster.

"That sounded pretty good," I say when he finishes.

He jumps back three steps, eyeing me with suspicion. I see the name Stevie Wonder carved into the face of the violin, along with felt-pen doodles.

"Oh, thank you very much," he says, obviously flattered. "Are you serious?"

"I'm not a musician," I answer. "But yes. It sounded good to me."

He is black, just beyond fifty, with butterscotch eyes that warm to the compliment. He is standing next to a shopping cart heaped over with all his belongings, and yet despite grubby, soiled clothing, there's a rumpled elegance about him. He speaks with a slight regional accent I can't place. Maybe he's from the Midwest or up near the Great Lakes, and he seems to have been told to always stand up straight, enunciate, carry himself with pride and respect others.

"I'm trying to get back in shape," he says. "But I'm going to get back in there, playing better. I just need to keep practicing."

"So you like Stevie Wonder?" I ask.

"Oh, yes, certainly. 'You Are the Sunshine of My Life.' 'My Cherie Amour.' I guess I shouldn't have written his name on my violin, though."

I write a column for the *Los Angeles Times*. The job is a little like fishing. You go out and drop a line, cast a net. I'm figuring this vagrant violinist is a column. Has to be.

"I'm in a hurry at the moment," I tell him, "but I'd like to come back and hear you play again."

"Oh, all right," he says, smiling appreciatively but with trepidation. He looks like a man who has learned to trust no one.

"Do you always play in this spot?" I ask.

"Yes," he says, pointing across the street with his bow to Pershing Square, in the heart of downtown Los Angeles. "I like to be near the Beethoven statue for inspiration."

This guy could turn out to be a rare find in a city of undiscovered gems, fiddling away in the company of Beethoven. I would drop everything if I could, and spend a few hours pulling the story out of him, but that will have to wait for another day. I've got another column lined up and not much time to shape it. The deadlines come at you without mercy, even in your dreams.

"I'll be back," I say.

He nods indifferently.

Back at the office I sweat out another column, scan the mail and clear the answering machine. I make a note on the yellow legal pad where I keep a list of possibilities.

Violin Man.

It's got potential. Who knows where it will go?

Part One

1

I can't get the image out of my head, this odd picture of grubby refinement. But when I go back to look for the violinist in Pershing Square, I come up empty. His disappearance only makes the mystery more provocative.

Who was he? Where did he go? What is his story?

Three weeks later, he's back, reappearing in the same spot, and I watch from across the street for a while before approaching. His playing is a little scratchy and tentative, but just like before, it's clear this is no beginner. There'd been some serious training in there, somewhere along the way. He doesn't appear to be playing for money, which seems strange for a homeless guy. He plays as if he's a student, oblivious to everyone around him, and this is a practice session.

Strange place to practice. The ground shakes when buses roar by, and his strings are barely audible in the orchestra of horns, trucks and sirens. I gaze at the tops of buildings adorned with gargoyles and grand cornices. Men and women move about, duty-bound, ignoring him for the most part as they disappear around corners and into entryways. The man plays on, a lone fiddler. He throws his head back, closes his eyes, drifts. A portrait of tortured bliss.

When he pauses, I move in.

"Hello," I say.

He jumps back, startled just as before.

"Do you remember me?" I ask.

"I remember your voice."

He's still suspicious of me, suspicious of everything around him, it seems. He says he was trying to remember a Tchaikovsky piece he once knew quite well, but now it is as elusive as the meaning of a dream. It's obvious that he's troubled in some way, like so many others who wander the streets as if they inhabit a different planet than the rest of us, wrapped in many-layered outfits to keep from coming unraveled. He's wearing a ratty blue sweater with a light brown T-shirt over it and the collar of a shirt spilling out over the top of it all. Wrapped around his neck, like a scarf, is a yellow terry-cloth towel. His pants hang low on his waist, fitted for a man three sizes bigger, and his grimy white sneakers have no laces.

He tells me his name is Nathaniel Anthony Ayers. From Cleveland. He's going to keep practicing until he's proud of what he hears, he says, and I tell him I might like to write about him for the *L.A. Times*.

"Seriously?" he asks. "You'd really want to write about me?"

"Why not?" I ask.

He's a handsome guy, lean and fit-looking, with a strong jaw and clean white teeth. He reminds me a little of Miles Davis. I ask where he lives and he says at the Midnight Mission, one of the biggest rescue operations on nearby Skid Row. Not inside, he specifies. But on the street, though he showers and takes some meals inside.

"Why not sleep inside?"

"Oh, no," he says. "I wouldn't want to do that."

I wonder how safe it can be for a man trying to reconnect with Tchaikovsky as drug dealers, prostitutes and hustlers work streets teeming with the lame and the afflicted. Skid Row is a dumping ground for inmates released from the nearby county jail, and it's a place where the sirens never stop screaming.

"Maybe I'll come by and visit you at the mission," I tell him.

He nods, but I can see he doesn't trust me. He tucks the violin back under his chin, eager to get back to his music, and I know that if this one ever pans out, it's going to take some time. I'll have to check back with him now and again until he's comfortable enough to open up. Maybe I could go on his rounds with him over the course of a day or so, see if anyone can help fill in the blanks in his story or explain his condition. As he begins to play, I wave good-bye, and he responds with a suspicious glance in my general direction.

Two weeks later, I go looking for him once more and he's disappeared again. I stroll over to the mission at Fourth and Los Angeles streets, where I see street people by the dozens, some of them drug-ravaged, some of them raving mad, some of them lying so still on the pavement it's hard to tell whether they're napping or waiting for a ride to the morgue.

I check with Orlando Ward, the public information man at

the Midnight. He tells me he's seen the violinist around, but doesn't know the backstory. And he hasn't seen him lately.

Now I'm worried that I've lost the column.

Weeks go by and I get distracted by other things, shoveling whatever I can find into that empty space on the page. And then one day while driving to work from my home in Silver Lake, a neighborhood five miles northwest of downtown, I cut through the Second Street tunnel and there he is, putting on a one-man concert in a location even noisier than the last one.

He remembers me this time.

"Where have you been?" I ask.

He says he's been around, here and there. Nowhere special.

A car whooshes by and his mind reels.

"Blue car, green car, white car," he says. "There goes a police car, and God is on the other side of that wall."

I nod, not knowing what to say. Maybe he's a little more un-reachable than I realized. Do I take notes for a column, or do I make a few calls to see if someone can come and help him?

"There goes Jacqueline du Pré," Nathaniel says, pointing at a woman a block away. "She's really amazing."

I tell him I doubt that it's the late cellist, who died in 1987.

Nathaniel says he isn't so sure.

"I don't know how God works," he tells me sincerely, with an expression that says anything is possible.

I scribble that down in my notebook, and I also copy what he's written on his shopping cart with a Magic Marker:

"Little Walt Disney Concert Hall—Beethoven."

I ask Nathaniel if he has moved to this location to be near the concert hall and he says no, he isn't even sure where Disney Hall is, exactly.

"Is it around here?" he asks.

"Right up the hill. The great big silvery building that looks like a schooner."

"Oh, that's it?"

He says he moved to this spot because he could see the Los Angeles Times Building two blocks away.

"Don't you work there?" he asks.

Having lived in Cleveland, New York and Los Angeles, Nathaniel tells me, it's reassuring to be able to look up at the L.A. Times Building and know where he is.

He plays for a while; we talk for a while, an experience that's like dropping in on a dream. Nathaniel takes nonsensical flights, doing figure eights through unrelated topics. God, the Cleveland Browns, the mysteries of air travel and the glory of Beethoven. He keeps coming back to music. His life's purpose, it seems, is to arrange the notes that lie scattered in his head.

I notice for the first time that his violin, caked with grime and a white chalky substance that looks like a fungus, is missing an important component or two.

"Your violin has only two strings," I say. "You're missing the other two."

Yes, he says. He's well aware.

"All I want to do is play music, and the crisis I'm having is right here. This one's gone," he says of the missing top string, "that one's gone, and this little guy's almost out of commission."

His goal in life, Nathaniel tells me, is to figure out how to re-

place the strings. But he got used to playing imperfect instruments
while taking music classes in Cleveland's public schools, and there's
a lot you can do, he assures me, with just two strings.

I notice while talking to him that someone has scrawled names
on the pavement where we're standing. Nathaniel says he did it
with a rock. The list includes Babe Ruth, Susan, Nancy, Kevin
and Craig.

"Whose names are those?" I ask.

Oh, those people, he says.

"Those were my classmates at Juilliard."

2

I half run back to the Los Angeles Times Building, a downtown landmark that squats on the better part of one square block kitty-corner from City Hall. For nearly four years, it has been my head-quarters, the place where I have sweat hundreds of columns for the California section. This is my seventh newspaper in a thirty-year career that included a four-year stint at *Time* magazine. Although I'm not much past fifty, there are days, to be honest, when I wonder how many more years I have left. Desire isn't the problem. The question is whether newspapers will still be relevant at a time when readers are flocking to the Internet and our most solid core of subscribers is slowly dying off, with newsroom cut-backs keeping pace.

The antidote for such fear and loathing is, of course, a good story. When you're in the chase, the adrenaline pumps, minutes seem like seconds, and in your single-minded state you are for all intents and purposes a zombie, ignorant of everything around you and capable of nothing but checking out the lead. I'm out of breath as I cut into the back entrance of the slab-gray Times Building, thinking all the while that Juilliard in Manhattan is one of the elite music schools in the world, and if Nathaniel really studied there, with a little more legwork I've got myself a good column. Though I had written thousands of stories in a career that included stops at the *Philadelphia Inquirer*, *Oakland Tribune* and *San Jose Mercury News*, I still came upon each one like a kid at an Easter egg hunt, as if I wasn't certain I'd ever find another.

One of the great joys of my job is the chance to hold the feet of public officials to the fire. I also love exposing the vanities of the rich and famous and delivering public floggings to corporate villains and self-important fools who deserve nothing less, but there is no satisfaction like the discovery of the story that sits right in front of you, so obvious it's practically invisible. A bum with a violin, living out of a shopping cart and worshipping a Beethoven statue, turns out to be a Juilliard alum. My chance encounter had affirmed a golden rule in journalism: everyone has a story, so get out of the office and talk to people. There's no telling what you might find.

My desk is on the third floor of the newsroom. Wisecracking hacks call the area Baja Metro because it's south of the main Metro section. The typical greeting to fellow journalists is a grunt or a "Hey," not much more, and I toss out a few before plopping into my chair and flipping my notebook onto the junk pile I live with. I Google Juilliard, which has no list of alums on its Web site. I call the number, leave a message for someone in publicity and e-mail my question as well. It's late in the day in New York and no one at Juilliard seems prepared to drop everything and investigate my query. I give it another try by phone and finally get an answer, but it isn't the one I'm looking for.

Sorry. There doesn't seem to be any record of a student by the name of Nathaniel Anthony Ayers.

Damn. There goes a good hook. If the poor soul is that delusional, he's even sicker than I thought. Is it dementia? Bipolar disorder? I'm no doctor, but I am able to diagnose the mild dread that is now washing over me, accompanied by a nervous stomach. These are the symptoms of a columnist with no column. Fortunately, I'm not scheduled to write today, and surely something will turn up by the next deadline. Something always does.

I reach for the yellow legal pad, but my list of column ideas seems warmed over, not a single clear-cut winner in the bunch. Maybe that's because I still can't get my mind off Nathaniel. I'm not a bad judge of people, a skill that comes from thousands of reads, and he seemed like a decent fellow, charismatic and compelling in his own way, climbing onto the stage each day at his Little Walt Disney Concert Hall. Juilliard or no, he still intrigued me, and his choice to move from the Beethoven statue to the tunnel struck me as peculiar. With very few pedestrians there, he wouldn't make much money and he'd never replace the two missing strings.

Wait a minute.

Did he move to the tunnel to be closer to me?

The very next day someone at Juilliard calls to say there's been an oversight. Yes, it turns out, there indeed once was a student at Juilliard by the name of Nathaniel Anthony Ayers. No additional information is readily available, not even the years he attended. But he is listed as an alum.

I hang up the phone and stand at my desk, looking for someone to share the news with. The guy went to Juilliard, I tell the
nearest reporter, Jim Rainey. I met this guy playing a crummy,
gunked-up violin with smudges and graffiti all over it, he tells me
he went to Juilliard and it checks out. Can you believe it? He's
over there now, chalking the names of his classmates onto the
pavement.

"That sounds like it's got some possibilities," says Rainey, a
master of deadpan.

I decide the story is too good to rush, so over the next couple
of weeks I jam a few easier columns into print while digging up
more details on Nathaniel's life. After I meet with him a few
more times, he no longer jumps back when I approach. He's a
little warmer each time. "Oh, Mr. Lopez," he says. "How are you
today?" I learn that there's one nonnegotiable rule with Nathaniel. While performing, he is an artist at work and does not appreciate being interrupted, a misstep that always draws a look of
scorn. Sometimes, while waiting for him to pause, I take stock of
the items crammed into his shopping cart. It's nothing less than
a work of art and clever engineering, with an astounding number
of items arranged in a precise manner. Blankets, a sleeping bag,
clothing, two yard-long sticks, a blue tarp, a water gun the size of
a small cannon, a hubcap, a single black boot. Five-gallon buckets
dangle off the cart like saddlebags and artificial flowers are fastened to the top of the heap for a home-sweet-home effect. In
his open violin case, which Nathaniel rests atop the cart while
playing, I see a small, empty white paper bag that bears the name
Studio City Music.

"Black man?" Hans Benning, the owner of Studio City Music,

asks when I call. "We do have a guy who plays with a badly beaten-up fiddle. He comes here every so often. He's very kind, very gentle and very proper. He's a delight.... He talks about Beethoven sonatas and then slips back into another world."

Yeah, that's my guy.

Whatever Nathaniel is playing at Second and Hill, it sounds brilliant at times and awful at others. Then again, he's missing two strings. I've got a good ear for pitch, but I'm no musician, and several years of guitar lessons many years ago didn't get me far. I wish now that I knew something about classical music so I could be a better judge of Nathaniel's work. But the music I love, and know a little bit about, is jazz. So I can only nod dumbly but appreciatively when he answers one of my questions.

"That was an idea I got from Ernest Bloch," he tells me. "B-L-O-C-H. Swiss-born composer who served as director of the Cleveland Institute of Music."

When I tell him how impressed I am that he studied at Juilliard, he's all modesty.

"I was there for a couple of years."

But only a tiny percentage of the world's greatest violinists could ever hope to get into Juilliard, I tell him, so he had to be a major talent.

"Oh, I didn't play violin," he says. "I played double bass."

"Then where'd you learn how to play violin?"

"I don't know how to play violin," he says. "I've been trying to teach myself, but it's difficult to transpose the music from bass to violin. It would help if I had some sheet music, but I don't know how to get my hands on any."

He tried the cello briefly after leaving Juilliard and loved it, he tells me, but the violin was easier to lug around in a shopping cart. There's no way to keep playing a big upright string bass, he says, while living on the streets. But he still has Saint-Saëns, Mozart, Brahms, Dvořák, Haydn and Beethoven in his head, so he tries to make something of their compositions on the two-string violin he claims to have bought at Motter's Music House in Cleveland many years ago.

I call Motter's, and Ron Guzzo, one of the managers, recalls the purchase. The violin was one of many instruments Nathaniel bought from him over a span of nearly twenty years, Guzzo tells me. He kept buying new ones because others were stolen from him on the streets of Cleveland. Nathaniel would get a job shoveling snow, Guzzo says, or working at a Wendy's, until he had saved enough to buy another instrument.

"As I understand it, he was at Juilliard and got sick, so he came back home," Guzzo says of Nathaniel, whom he knew by Anthony—his middle name—or Tony. The staff at Motter's was always amazed at how nimbly Nathaniel switched from one instrument to another. "He'd sit out in our parking lot on a nice day playing the cello, and we'd wonder where the heck that was coming from. It was Tony."

Getting sick at Juilliard was a subject I didn't know how to bring up with Nathaniel, nor did I know whether I should. Is it too personal? Will it upset him? Can I trust the answer of a man who has mental problems? I need to know more for my column, though, so I ask if it was true he left Juilliard before finishing his studies.

"Oh, yeah, I bombed out of there," he says.

"What happened?"

"I don't even remember, it's so far back now."

I ask if he has any relatives I could speak to, and Nathaniel recites the memorized phone number of his uncle Howard and aunt Willa in Cleveland. They refer me to Nathaniel's younger sister Jennifer, a social worker in Atlanta, and there's relief in her voice when I tell her I've met her brother.

"Is he okay?" she asks in a trembling voice, saying he hasn't been heard from in years.

It was the fall semester of 1972, his third year at Juilliard, and Nathaniel had been tormented by months of confusion, anxiety and hallucinations. One night, at the Upper East Side apartment of a Juilliard classmate and his fiancée, Nathaniel began shedding his clothes for no apparent reason. The classmate and his fiancée, alarmed by the bizarre behavior, couldn't get Nathaniel to stop disrobing. He wasn't angry or aggressive, but he seemed to be under a dark spell, and as he grew more distant, his friends became all the more frightened and concerned. His classmate didn't know what else to do but call the police, and Nathaniel, twenty-one years old, was wheeled away to the psychiatric emergency room at Bellevue Hospital. The diagnosis was paranoid schizophrenia, and his life, as he had lived it until then, was over. So, too, were his hopes of a career in music.

Jennifer watched helplessly as her big brother, the smart and smooth-talking man of the arts, drifted in and out of treatment for years back in Cleveland, trying medication, counseling and shock therapy, none of which helped for long. The fastidious dresser became a disheveled wreck who wandered the streets with musical instruments, slept in the woods and carved names into trees. He was incoherent, angry and prone to violent outbursts that broke their mother's heart a thousand times over. Floria, who was busy running a Cleveland beauty salon, would cook for him, clean for him, shower him with love and keep giving him yet another chance, only to have Nathaniel trash the furniture, smash lamps and mutilate the walls with nonsensical drawings. And yet for all the abuse, Nathaniel adored his mother and felt utterly lost when she died in 2000 after a lengthy illness.

And so he headed west, looking for the father who had abandoned the family when Nathaniel was just nine or ten. They'd been out of touch for so many years, though, that Nathaniel didn't know that his father, a retired Los Angeles trash truck driver, had already resettled in a retirement community in Las Vegas. Nathaniel stayed briefly in the garage of his father's daughter from a second marriage, then decided he wanted to be on his own in downtown Los Angeles. He had been wandering the streets for several years when, on that day in Pershing Square, our paths crossed for the first time.

A jet flies over downtown Los Angeles, making the big swing before looping back around on its descent to LAX. Nathaniel gazes up, childlike, then turns to me, one eyebrow arched, and asks if I'm flying the plane.

It's a chilling moment that offers a glimmer of the delusion he lives with. I wonder if I should respond, but I don't. I wonder if I should be scared, but I'm not. I'm too curious to be scared, and I'd like to know more about how a black kid growing up in the sixties—when the civil rights movement and Vietnam War divided the country and cities like Cleveland were on fire—beat the odds and ended up in Juilliard's classical music program. Was he a child prodigy? Were his mother and father musicians or aficionados who filled the house with the sounds of Beethoven and Ernest Bloch, B-L-O-C-H? If not for the breakdown, would Nathaniel be up the hill in a tuxedo, playing with the L.A. Philharmonic, instead of scratching away down here at his Little Walt Disney Concert Hall?

I can't help but think of the heartbreak for his family, and I wonder if there were clues earlier in his life that something might not be right. Or does the madness come up in a person randomly and without warning? Maybe it's all too much to expect to be able to pry out of him. Who am I, after all, to make his story mine?

Someone with deadlines, I remind myself. Someone who knows a good story when he sees one. Someone who imagines a reader pausing over the story of Nathaniel's descent from lofty aspiration and saying, "There, but for the grace of God, go I."

Well, Nathaniel tells me, there was Joseph Russo. He was a good friend. And Joseph Bongiorno was another bass player at Juillard. B-O-N-G-I-O-R-N-O. I ask if he knows whether they or any other classmates stuck with music.

He's been out of touch and doesn't know where everyone ended up, he says. But "a kid named Yo-Yo Ma" has done pretty well for himself.

"You knew Yo-Yo Ma?"

Not really, Nathaniel says. The cellist was in a different league even back then.

"But we played in the same orchestra," Nathaniel says. "I was in awe of the youngster."

He tells me his bass teacher was Homer M-E-N-S-C-H, who, in his nineties, was still teaching at Juilliard.

"He had the talent, that was for sure," Mensch says of Nathaniel, asking how things have turned out for the kid from Cleveland. I tell him Nathaniel lives on Skid Row and plays a violin that's missing two strings, and the line goes quiet.

"Give him my very best," says Mensch. "I would certainly like to hear from him."

If I want to talk to the man who knows him best, Nathaniel tells me, I should call Harry Barnoff. In Cleveland. That's B-A-R-N-O-F-F.

"I'll try to find a number," I tell Nathaniel.

With his index finger, he writes out the ten-digit number on his imaginary blackboard.

"Do you call him often?" I ask.

"I haven't spoken to him in years."

I dial the number from my office and a woman answers.

"Is this the Harry Barnoff residence?" I ask.

"Yes," she says. "This is his daughter."

Harry Barnoff recently retired after playing double bass in the Cleveland Orchestra for forty-six years. Nathaniel had been referred to him as a young teenager, and Barnoff was his teacher and friend for many years. When I describe Nathaniel's current situation, Barnoff is so distraught he begins to weep.

"Please," the musician pleads, relieved to hear that Nathaniel is alive, if not entirely well, "you have got to tell him how much I think of him and that I still remember what a wonderful musician he was."

He was not always the best student, recalls Barnoff, who tutored Nathaniel at the Cleveland Music School Settlement, a nonprofit in the University Circle neighborhood of Cleveland. Nathaniel blew off assignments and had trouble focusing, according to Barnoff, who wonders if Nathaniel was too talented for his own good. Barnoff had never seen a student go months without practice, as Nathaniel sometimes did, then pick up an instrument and get such a great sound out of it.

"You've really got something here," he told Nathaniel, pleading with him to respect and nurture his gift.

That combination of flattery and faith got Nathaniel's attention. In his late teens, Nathaniel announced with equal parts arrogance and admiration that he wanted to be like Mr. Barnoff and play in a major orchestra. Barnoff was reluctant to set him up for disappointment. Sure, he told Nathaniel, you've got talent, but it takes more than that. "You've got to make music your life. You've got to practice, practice, practice." In his own case, Barnoff told Nathaniel, he had worked hard enough to make it to this fancy New York school called Juilliard.

"I want to go to Juilliard, too," Nathaniel told Barnoff.

Barnoff recalls that while Cleveland was rupturing, with police in riot gear dragging away protesters, fires raging and cars being overturned, Nathaniel was often in his cocoon at the Settlement school. A change had come over the young man. He was more mature and less restless, and after high school, he won a scholarship to the music school at Ohio University. Barnoff was thrilled for his protégé, but Nathaniel was still after a bigger prize. Halfway through his freshman year at Ohio U., he flew to Juilliard for an audition.

"Next thing I knew," Barnoff says, his voice breaking, "he got a scholarship."

I bring him two new violin strings from Studio City Music and Nathaniel breaks them in on Mendelssohn, Brahms and Beethoven. "I can't thank you enough," he says. "It's an absolute dream here, and I notice that everyone is smiling. The sun is out all day, and the nights are cool and serene."

I watch patiently as he strings the violin and jabbers on good-naturedly, keyed up about playing a properly equipped instrument. Just up the hill, Disney Hall is a great landed ship with mercury sails, a gleaming hallucination on the skyline. Down here, cars streak through the Second Street tunnel, trucks rumble, sirens blare, and Nathaniel begins to play, slicing through the madness. His eyes are closed, and in his shuttered world there is order, logic, sanity, sweet relief. If only for a while.

3

The Sunday paper slaps my driveway with a thud that opens one eye, pays the mortgage and puts thirty years of work on the line. Last week's columns are nonexistent, zapped by a constant, white-hot beam of news and information that blurs history. You're only as good or bad as your latest attempt to make some connection with the world, and Nathaniel's story hits like nothing I've written before. In the time it takes to read an e-mail, two more arrive, an endless stream that snakes through lunch and then dinner and spills into the next day. I know it's a compelling story, and the pitch-perfect headline, written by copy editor Saji Mathai, has helped draw attention to it:

He's Got the World on Two Strings

But the response exceeds my expectations and has me wondering what it is about the story that I've underestimated. The answer is in the responses. Readers see the tale of a man, stunned by a blow thirty years earlier, who carries on with courage and dignity, spirit intact. It's as simple as that, with one wrinkle. My serendipitous meeting with Nathaniel is seen as his second chance. Am I aware of this program or that? Do I know about the new generation of antipsychotic medication that could change his life? Would I please print my address so people can send strings and unused instruments dug out of dusty attics? Forgotten for years, Nathaniel now has a rooting section. Four readers offer to pack up and ship violins. A violin maker offers to build one from scratch. And a man named Al Rich sends this:

> *Steve,*
>
> *I'm the CEO of the Pearl River Piano Group America, Ltd. We are the western world arm of the Guanghou Pearl River Piano Group, the largest piano builder and second largest musical instrument builder in the world. Our American office is in Ontario, California. This morning I read your article about the street violinist in L.A. and of course was moved by your story.*

Rich says he's sending a student-model cello and violin by express mail, and when I've read through all these offers, I rush out to Second and Hill to deliver the news.

"He's going to send a cello?" Nathaniel asks of the Pearl River CEO, his face pinched with doubt. He hasn't read the column, and he's having trouble making sense of his sudden turn of fortune.

"A cello and a violin," I tell him, "and several other people say they're sending violins."

Nathaniel seems to be studying me for signs that I'm real, and not some cruel illusion.

"People are awfully generous," he says, but shadows of doubt fill his eyes, and something is troubling him. "I can't cover that," he says, shaking his head.

"You don't have to pay them anything," I say. "These are people who read my story about you in the paper and think you sound like a decent guy. They don't want anything but the pleasure of knowing they helped a fellow musician."

This seems to bring him around to the idea. If they're musicians, they're part of a brotherhood, and Nathaniel is obliged to respect their sensibilities.

"How are they going to send them to me?" he asks, very much aware that he is cut off from ordinary connections, living without an address or P.O. box.

"They're sending them to me and I'll bring them to you. It should happen in the next week or so."

He nods his approval, but I can tell he doesn't trust me. And why should he? A gray-bearded, balding columnist has suddenly parachuted into his life, promising enough free instruments for him to start his own chamber orchestra. Suspicion, if not paranoia, is a perfectly logical response.

In the days that follow, Nathaniel sets up near the tunnel every morning by eight or nine, meticulously unloading his shopping cart on the patio-sized slab that serves as his stage. But the first order of business is for him to compulsively pick up every speck of dirt, debris and tobacco by hand. He lectures against foul language and the scourge of drugs, but cigarette butts are an obsession, a pox, a menace, and he plucks them off the pavement with pinched fingers and disgustedly dumps them in trash cans, as if it has been left to him alone to save the world from the spreading plague. On occasion he drops everything to dart into the street for a fresh butt tossed from a moving vehicle, his flat face wrinkled into a scowl as he denounces the nicotine junkies whose weakness rots the underpinnings of civil society. His mad dash between cars is a spectacle, not just for the inherent danger, but because he sometimes scrambles about in a full-length velvet burgundy-colored robe, looking like some kind of fantastical wizard. Other times he wears a black trash bag safety-pinned over his back and around his neck, the caped, clean-streets crusader of downtown Los Angeles.

With the approach of spring, the morning sun rises out of East L.A. and angles down hard on the concrete alcove at the mouth of the tunnel, where Nathaniel has taken to propping up two cardboard signs announcing his current musical interests.

"Bach and Brahms," says one.

"Beethoven's Eighth," says the other.

He has painted them with black hair dye. Nearby, he sets a Japanese magazine on the ground, saying it's a tribute to Little Tokyo, a pint-sized commercial neighborhood just a few blocks to the east. Everyone there looks like Yo-Yo Ma, he tells me.

"Did you get the cello yet?" he asks more than once with childlike anticipation. "The cello and the violins?"

Not yet, Nathaniel. Any day now.

Trust me.

He nods, unable to mask disappointment or doubt.

If he's got bugs in his pants, he tells me. If he's just dug a hole in the ivy bed to bury human feces from tunnel dwellers who didn't have the decency to use proper facilities, he tells me. Nathaniel is refreshingly uninhibited and without pretense, uttering whatever pops into his head. There are no filters, and no wall between the real and imagined. A simple question about his love of Beethoven sends him on a flight through unhinged thoughts that float through his mind like wind-driven clouds.

"Cleveland doesn't have the Beethoven statue. That's a military-oriented city, occupied, preoccupied, with all the military figures of American history, the great soldiers and generals, but you don't see the musicians on parade, although you do have Severance Hall, Cleveland Music School Settlement, Ohio University Bobcats, Buckeyes of Ohio State. All the great soldiers are there from the United States military, World War Two, Korean War, whereas in Los Angeles you have the LAPD, Los Angeles County Jail, *Los Angeles Times*, Mr. Steve Lopez. That's an army, right? The *L.A. Times*? Los Angeles is sloped downward like a valley, Santa Monica Mountains, downtown Los Angeles, Honolulu. I haven't seen the ocean in Los Angeles. There's supposed to be an ocean, the Pacific, but this is not ocean terrain in the downtown area. You don't see the military statues like you have in Cleveland, where those are the leaders of the city and they have their army all over town with lots of horses. Cleveland Browns, Los Angeles Rams, those are armies, too, military regimentation, experimentation, with Mr. Roman Gabriel as quarterback, Roman, Romans, Roman Empire, Colonel Sanders, Mr. Roman Gabriel designing a play in his dreams. Look. There go all the wide receivers down the street. This little guy here is the quarterback of the orchestra, this violin which I purchased some years back at Motter's Music in Cleveland, Ohio. A cello can back this guy up with the same moves, but the cello is not the concert-master. It's this youngster here that leads the way. Itzhak Perlman, Jascha Heifetz, they're like gods to me. I wish I had that talent, but if I practiced for the next ten thousand years I could never be that good. In Cleveland you cannot play music in winter because of the snow and ice, and that's why I prefer Los Angeles, the Beethoven city, where you have this sunshine and if it rains you can go into the tunnel and play to your heart's content. I am absolutely flabbergasted by that statue. It knocks me out that someone as great as Beethoven is the leader of Los Angeles. Do you have any idea who put him there?"

Good Lord. What have I gotten myself into?

Nathaniel delivers this and other broken streams of consciousness with the enthusiasm and charm of a smooth conversationalist, emphasis here, a smile or hand gesture there, and no earthly awareness of the scrambled nature of the offering. Sometimes I come upon him in full conversation with someone who isn't there, a fluid, animated back-and-forth with the wall or with a tree or with nothing at all. I don't know if he's answering voices or simply uttering his every thought. I know little about his illness, how it works, what to do or whom to ask.

In other words, I've got a problem. Several instruments are in transit to my office, and I haven't given any thought to what I might do with them when they arrive. Nathaniel would need to attach a U-Haul trailer to his orange buggy to haul them around. I suppose I'll bring him the cello and maybe one of the new violins and hold on to the rest of them in my office. But there's another little problem I've never considered, and it's now filling me with dread. A man who lives outdoors and sleeps in a dangerous, crime-infested netherworld of prowling addicts and thieves will be a nice fat target for a mugging. It's not as if he can conceal instruments on the buggy. I consider keeping all the instruments at my office and having him come by when he wants to play one, but it's out of the question. I'm not there half the time, and when I am, I've got no time to play music-room monitor.

I've set a trap for myself without knowing it, and readers aren't letting me forget it. The responses still pour in, with well-wishers wondering how Nathaniel is doing and when they'll get to read an update. A column is a personal take, and as such, it's less dispassionate than a straight news story. But in telling Nathaniel's story, I have unwittingly taken on some responsibility for his welfare, a job I am clearly, demonstrably and undeniably unqualified for. Sure, I intend to update the story. But I have no intention of adopting a homeless, middle-aged, mentally ill man. I've got a wife, Alison, and a two-year-old daughter, Caroline, and I don't get to spend as much time with them as I'd like, thanks to a schedule that often gets me home after Caroline is down for the night.

I mention my predicament to a colleague named Tom Curwen, who has been the *Times'* assistant book editor and later became editor of the Outdoors section. He tells me another of our colleagues recognized one of the many panhandlers outside the Times Building as a former classmate and called Lamp Community, a downtown Los Angeles agency that works with mentally ill homeless people. The panhandler is now doing quite well in treatment.

I'm vaguely familiar with Lamp, having once met the ex-director, Mollie Lowery, a former nun. But I don't know much about the program and have never met the two Lamp employees who answer my call for help and arrive at Second and Hill to have a look at Nathaniel. He's too focused on his music to notice the arrival of Shannon Murray, the assistant director, and Patricia Lopez, a program manager. The three of us stand several feet away, taking in the concert, and when he takes a break I introduce everyone. Nathaniel is gracious and charming. He repeats Murray's and Lopez's names several times, committing them to memory. He seems to be under the impression that Patricia Lopez is my wife.

I tell Nathaniel I boasted about his talent, and that Murray and Lopez have schlepped about ten city blocks to come see for themselves. He gives a shy shrug, then tucks the violin under his chin, blocks out the roar of traffic and leaves the known world. He scratches around a bit, chasing after ideas that aren't quite coming together, but then, as always, he finds a passage that works like a drug and the music pushes him free of all distraction. Eyes closed, head tilted to the heavens, he's gone.

So, I whisper to the two visitors, do you think you can help him?

Murray pauses before answering. She's watching Nathaniel intently, as if studying a Cubist painting. I'm curious to know her every thought, her diagnosis, her prognosis, her prescription. She's young, maybe not yet forty, but has twenty years of experience with cases like this.

You know, she says, Lamp tries to accomplish two things, among many others. It tries to help its clients make social connections in a supportive setting, and also to come up with a mission or a goal, along with a plan to realize it. Nathaniel, it seems, already has an advocate and trusted acquaintance, namely me. And he has a mission—his music—that is nothing less than a consuming passion. In some ways, Murray says, Nathaniel would be considered a success story at Lamp.

Except, of course, that he is more than a little bit crazy by popular definition. There has to be something they can do for him. Isn't there?

Murray and Lopez compliment Nathaniel when he's done playing, and he responds with an Aw, shucks, clearly reveling in the glory of his growing fan club. But when they tell him to stop by Lamp if he ever needs anything, he winces, saying he doesn't think that's going to happen.

I wince, too, wondering, Why not?

Murray and Lopez tell Nathaniel to keep the option in mind as they begin to leave.

Wait a minute. That's it?

I'm not sure what I was expecting, but it was something more concrete than a casual suggestion that Nathaniel stop by Lamp if he happens to be in the neighborhood. I suppose I imagined them whisking him off to a place where he'd be on some kind of medication and sleeping under a roof as he transitioned to a new, more productive life. Of course, I know that's not an overnight process, but isn't that all the more reason to get things going as soon as possible?

Murray and Lopez tell me they'll have someone drop by on occasion to try to bring Nathaniel around to the idea of coming in for help. But if it has taken several visits for Nathaniel to get comfortable with me, how long will it take someone else?

When the Lamp emissaries depart, I feel abandoned and alone, and Nathaniel is doing nothing to lift my spirits.

"I am *not* going over there," he says with finality and defiance.

"But they're just trying to help," I tell him.

"Yeah, I understand that, but I don't need help."

"It's just a place to get a sandwich and take a shower. Shannon and Patricia seemed nice enough, didn't they?"

"Yeah, but I don't need the hassles I'd have to deal with going all the way over there with all of that nonsense. This isn't Cleveland, Ohio. It's a Beethoven town that doesn't have all of that snow and ice. *Los Angeles Times*. Roman Gabriel. Jackie Robinson. I like it right here in the tunnels, where I can play all day and nobody's going to bother me."

In all my years of columnizing, never have I run into unintended consequences of this magnitude. I'm on a street corner arguing with a paranoid schizophrenic, and because I don't know what to say next, I say good-bye.

"Um, Mr. Lopez?" Nathaniel calls after me. "You think the cello and violins are still coming?"

A newspaper column is the perfect job for an impatient man with a short attention span. There's little time to mull things over. You take on one subject and boom, you're on to the next like a hit-and-run driver. But Nathaniel has lured me into a cul-de-sac. Impatience, fortunately, is not my only flaw. I'm stubborn, too. So he thinks he's going to blow off Lamp after Murray and Lopez were kind enough to come offer him help? We'll see about that.

I call Patricia Lopez when I get back to my office and ask if she'll go in with me on my devious little plan. When the instruments arrive, I'm going to tell Nathaniel they're all his, but they're going to have to be stored at Lamp. I'll say the donors and I want to make sure that both the instruments and Nathaniel are safe. I'm thinking he'll do whatever it takes to get his hands on the new instruments, and his visits to Lamp will eventually open him to the idea of joining their treatment and housing programs.

Patricia Lopez is on board. She says they'll find a place to lock up the instruments for him, and he'll be free to play on Lamp property but not beyond.

It's simple. It's subversive. It's ingenious.

4

The instruments arrive. First one violin—which the owner has enclosed in a Sears chain-saw box—then another and another, and then comes the shipment from Mr. Rich of the Pearl River Piano Group. The cello is in a box roughly my height, and I tear it open to find the handsome new instrument encased in a dark blue nylon sock. Mr. Rich said it wasn't a high-quality cello, but to my untrained eye it's a masterful work of art, with sensual curves and dark robust wood with a warm honey finish that's smooth to the touch. I wish I knew how to get music out of it, and I find myself anticipating Nathaniel's reaction and envying his talent.

Learning how to play an instrument has always been near the top of my to-do list, but what are the chances now? There's little downtime with a column and a two-year-old, and after reading *Goldilocks and the Three Bears* and going through half a bottle of wine with dinner on an average evening, imagining a day when I join

Nathaniel on the Elgar Cello Concerto is not a vision but a hallucination. I'm at the point where the things on your to-do list get transferred to a should-have-done list, and one reason I write a column is for the privilege of vicariously sampling other worlds, dropping in with my passport, my notebook and my curiosity. I may carp about feeling cornered by Nathaniel, as is my right as a curmudgeonly columnist, but there's nothing boring about the adventure I'm on. I am the inadequately educated grandson of grocery store owners who arrived in California in the 1920s from Spain on my father's side and Italy on my mother's side, learning something about survival and fine music from a schizophrenic African-American man who grew up in East Cleveland.

New cello in one hand, new violin in the other, I stride through the newsroom, out the back door of the *Times* and up Second Street to Hill. My thinking is that if I take the instruments straight to Lamp without his seeing them first, Nathaniel may never go there on a blind date. But if he gets to first see the instruments and feel them in his hands, he'll go where love takes him. I stop for the light on the corner by the Kawada Hotel and see him up by the tunnel. It's mid-morning and he has been playing for two hours, but he stops when he spots me. He's a child at Christmas, his expression half delight and half relief. I've done it. I've come through for him, just as I said I would. I'm golden now, an angel in khakis and Rockports.

"I saw you flying around," Nathaniel says, "giving gifts."

I hand him Alfred Rich's business card. He studies it, one more detail tossed into the whirl and committed to memory for life. Then he places the card atop the blue tarp draped over his shopping cart. On one knee, he peeks inside the violin case and speaks of "the little rascal" asleep in there. He's smitten, and here's my chance.

"Mr. Rich wants you to know these are your instruments to play as often and as long as you please," I tell him, surprised by how easily the white lie comes. "But he wants you to keep them at Lamp and so do I. We don't want you to get mugged out here."

Nathaniel's eyes are incapable of hiding any emotion. They bulge from deep sockets, wildly expressive, and it's clear my proviso has not set well with him.

"I can handle myself out here. It's not like I haven't been mugged before," he argues, adding that he will "fight to the death to defend these instruments."

Terrific. I might as well just whack him myself and get it over with. That would be better than lying awake at night waiting for the call informing me that Nathaniel is laid up in a hospital, beaten senseless for the instruments I personally delivered to him.

"That's the deal," I say firmly, seeing no alternative but to stand my ground. "Why don't you test out the instruments for a little while and then I'll drive them over to Lamp, where they'll always be yours and no one else's."

He doesn't answer. He's discovered the cello.

"Oh my gosh," he gasps, carefully lifting and cradling the instrument as if it were a newborn child.

"It's beautiful," I agree.

Nathaniel immediately goes about assembling the cello, stationing the bridge just so and carefully drawing the strings up over virgin bones. I notice a spider-sized gold pin on his shirt—a pin of an angel playing violin. Flies buzz over the adjacent bed of ivy and around the buckets that dangle from his shopping cart, and traffic is a broken roar, whoosh, whoosh, rumble. Nathaniel tightens the strings, alternating between C, G, D and A, gradually pulling the stretch out of them. He takes an amber bulb of resin and dusts his new bow as he goes through a list of master cellists. Pablo Casals. Yo-Yo Ma. Jacqueline du Pré.

"And then there's the coolest, calmest cucumber of all time, Janos Starker," Nathaniel says of the Hungarian-born musician.

He's almost giddy, yammering as he often does but in a brighter mood and with greater control than usual, bubbling with images that are simultaneously daffy and brilliant.

"Putting resin on your bow," he says as he dusts away, "is like feeding your parakeet. A bow needs resin in the same way a police car needs prisoners."

And in the same way a columnist needs material. I scribble Nathaniel's musings in my spiral notebook, trying to keep up with a running soliloquy that is somewhat reminiscent of Joseph Mitchell's Professor Sea Gull character. In Mitchell's famed discoveries for *The New Yorker* magazine, Joe Gould, aka Jonathan Sea Gull, was a Bowery bohemian, urban philosopher, historian and unpublished writer twenty-six years into *An Oral History of Our Time,* a tattered manuscript he carried around while talking to pigeons and otherwise annoying those who dismissed him as a bum and a loon, in part for his occasional impersonation of a sea gull. But e. e. cummings had befriended Professor Sea Gull and William Saroyan had written that "no writer except Joe Gould seemed to have imagination enough to understand that if the worst came to the worst you didn't need to have any form at all. You didn't need to put what you had to say into a poem, an essay, a story, or a novel. All you had to do was say it."

Or, in Nathaniel's case, play it.

The cello is inspected, strung and ready for its maiden voyage. Nathaniel pulls out the webbed orange Driftwood Dairy crate he keeps on the bottom shelf of his shopping cart. He spreads a tarp before him to keep the end pin of the cello from making contact with the ground, saying he is determined to let no harm come to his new instrument. He's ready now, riding the dairy crate and straddling the instrument, but just as he begins to play, a woman who lives in the tunnel stands before him with something to say.

"It's always so relaxing to hear you play," she says.

Nathaniel takes the compliment well, even when it appears that the woman might be hustling him.

"I'm starving," she says, calling herself Estella. "I need a ninety-nine-cent hamburger, and a spider bit me. Look at this."

Nathaniel, who collects an occasional quarter or dollar bill tossed his way by a passerby, offers her a buck. But he's concerned about the bite on her leg, and carefully sets his cello aside to have a closer look. He offers Estella his dairy crate as a seat and leans in to examine an infected, nasty-looking wound. Her shin has grown a lump the size of a golf ball.

"I've got bugs that bite me inside my trousers," Nathaniel says while another homeless man emerges from the tunnel to speculate on the type of spider that has inflicted the damage, postulating that the wound suggests the work of a brown spider. Brown spiders, the stranger says, are on the prowl, the nasty buggers. These bites have to be taken care of, he advises, because a festering, untreated wound will soon be crawling with maggots.

Before too much longer, the Tortilla Flat confab breaks up with the woman on her way to get that ninety-nine-cent hamburger and Nathaniel back to the business at hand, settling again onto the Driftwood Dairy crate with his legs wrapped around the cello. His first offering is a Beethoven cello sonata, and this drab concrete corner of downtown Los Angeles, with its nearby settlement of bug-bitten denizens and moving clouds of noxious vehicle exhaust, is transformed into a place of lilting repose. The cello lets forth a deeper cry than the violin did, and it's better equipped to compete with the sound of wheels turning. It's been years since Nathaniel has held a cello in his hands, and he never had more than a few lessons after letting go of the double bass, so he stumbles at times and doubles back to rework phrases. But he looks natural and rather pleased with this first effort. I tell him it sounds terrific even though I can hear as many misses as hits, with the new strings losing their tune as they go slack.

Next comes Ernest Bloch's *Rhapsody for Cello,* which begins as a slow, poetic lament. Nathaniel's bow is a fluid and obedient slave, his fingers dancing ballet on the fresh-varnished neck, and the music cuts him off from noise, worry, fear, illness. I could watch for hours, but I've got work to do back at the office. This is when I'm supposed to play the bad guy and take the instrument away, but I can't do it. He's in such a state of ecstasy, I can't bring myself to break the mood. I tell him he can play a little while longer and then I'll be back to drive the instruments over to Lamp. At the moment he's too engrossed to argue the point.

At my computer, I do a little research on Ernest Bloch. "The cello represents a meditative voice, tragically alone," Bloch wrote of the rhapsody Nathaniel was just playing. I'm discovering, though, that Nathaniel isn't alone. Music is an anchor, a connection to great artists, to history and to himself. His head is filled with mixed signals, a frightening jumble of fractured meaning, but in music there is balance and permanence. The notes of *Rhapsody* sit on the staff as they did ninety years ago, precisely where Bloch left them. The work of Nathaniel's beloved Beethoven has endured through parts of three centuries and will last beyond our time. Music is a meditation, a reverie, a respite from madness. It is his way to be alone without fear.

After a few hours of work back at my office, I find Nathaniel as I left him, plopped on the dairy crate and in the embrace of music. He won't like what I'm about to do, but I don't see an alternative. It's possible he's already been scoped out by someone intent on grabbing the new cello.

I haven't given any consideration to what I might do if he resists, but I know the terms of the relationship are changing here and now. I am no longer a benign presence, the affable new guy in his life who brings casual conversation and occasional gifts, asking nothing in return. I can see that on some level he, too, senses this shift. He pulls the cello close to his body and looks at me with pleading eyes, as if I have arrived on the scene to kidnap his firstborn.

"I haven't really heard the instrument yet," he protests. "I'm just getting to know it."

"You can keep playing over at Lamp," I say, and I try convincing him it makes more sense to be in a quiet place.

"This is the perfect music environment," he insists, motioning toward the mouth of the tunnel as if it were the stage of the Hollywood Bowl. He knows Lamp is on Skid Row, where people will be swarming, standing in front of him while he tries to play and tossing cigarette butts at his feet.

I fall back on suggesting it's time for a break. He's been playing since the crack of dawn.

"Eight hours seems like two minutes when you're having fun," Nathaniel says. "Mr. Rich has given me a new lease on life."

Okay, the negotiations have ended. I tell Nathaniel this is the deal he's agreed to as I reach for the violin. He isn't happy, but he's done battling. I load the instruments into the trunk of my car and Nathaniel watches as if he might never see them again. I tell him to start pushing his cart across downtown to Skid Row and I'll wait for him at Lamp, so he can see exactly where his instruments are going to be kept.

Downtown Los Angeles disintegrates rapidly as you head east. In just a few blocks, business suits and corporate towers give way to a ten-block grid of streets littered with rejects and discards. Near Lamp, people by the hundreds roam trashed streets without purpose, camp in tents and boxes, or lie sprawled on the pavement as if they're dead. Some of them are filthy and insane, some are junkies or merely destitute, and still others are defending turf and trolling for trouble. It's chaos and collapse everywhere I look, with dead rats splattered flat on asphalt and the air spiked with drafts of decaying food, urine, vomit and misery. None of this is new to me, but I'm seeing it with fresh eyes now that I've got a personal investment here.

I stop my car and imagine Nathaniel pushing his cart through the squalor with a head full of beautiful music. Police are making an arrest at Sixth and San Julian, with a young black man in handcuffs against a wall. A woman sits in the middle of the street screaming. A siren wails as paramedics pull out of Station 9. Near the entrance to Lamp, two men argue about nothing, on the verge of flying fists. I walk through a courtyard and up to the second floor, where Patricia Lopez has found a place to keep Nathaniel's new cello and violin.

Lamp has thirty beds upstairs for chronically mentally ill people who are ready to come in and work with counselors and therapists to plot the next step. Might this one day be Nathaniel's new home? I'm getting ahead of myself. I tell Patricia Lopez I don't know whether Nathaniel will show.

It takes time, she tells me.

How much time?

Days, weeks, sometimes months.

Weeks or months?

I'm a newspaper columnist. We solve problems and move on. We've got deadlines.

5

A *month goes by.* The instruments are still in storage, untouched. I'm in my office one day, adding and subtracting columns from the list on the yellow pad, when my phone rings.

"I have some good news," says Shannon Murray. "Nathaniel is in the courtyard, playing his cello."

Though I'd nearly given up hope, a month doesn't seem so long now that I'm hurrying across Skid Row to catch the show. The concert is still in full swing when I get there, and I stand motionless for a moment, trying to restrain the urge to run up and pat Nathaniel on the back. He's wrapped around the cello, coaxing all the sound he can get out of his new instrument. He acknowledges my presence and I nod approvingly but choose not to interrupt him. He has an audience of about a dozen people, not that everyone is riveted, or even awake.

The courtyard is about forty feet square, with terraced benches on one side, a couple of picnic tables, and a steady flow of people moving in and out of the adjacent building or coming in off the street in search of food, bathrooms and company. Nathaniel's soothing music is a nice touch at so busy an asylum, and it's appropriately schizophrenic, too, lovely at times and lost at others.

"He can't play," one man sniffs, shaking his head.

I'm hoping this kind of thing doesn't drive Nathaniel away. It's not that I'm certain this is the right program for him, and to be honest, I can understand why anyone would want to avoid coming here. I just need to get on with my life and have some assurance that he's in a place where he can get help. But as he predicted with scorn, people are smoking and flicking cigarettes here and there, and hard-boiled arguments can be heard from the homeless encampment on the street just a few feet beyond the courtyard doors. The courtyard itself is a hall of horrors, with every manner of biological disturbance and human breakdown on display, even though most people appear docile, if not sedated. There's incessant muttering and squawks from bedraggled souls, there are angry stare-downs that tip toward violence and there is a stunning array of Halloween-like getups, one woman dressed as a flapper, another in white-face, a man with a pair of pants a good eight inches too short.

"Yeah, like this family can EVER have a SENSible converSAtion," one young man barks to his imaginary relatives as a Lamp employee emerges from the lobby of the building to announce the start of a class inside:

"Anger management! Anybody here want to go to anger management?"

I wait for relative calm and then dial Nathaniel's sister Jennifer in Atlanta. I've been keeping her abreast of my efforts to help her brother and waiting for just the right moment to have them chat by phone for the first time in several years. Jennifer squeals with delight when I tell her where her brother is and what he's doing. Yes, she says, of course she'd like to speak to him. I hand Nathaniel the phone and he looks at it with puzzlement. At fifty-four, it might be the first time he's ever used a cell phone.

"I'm very fond of you, too," he tells his little sister after a short conversation, and then he's back to his music.

A white-haired woman named Carol seems to be one of Nathaniel's more appreciative fans, taking in the concert from a bench against one wall. She has read about him in my column and was surprised to find him playing at Lamp, where she has lived for several years. She says she told Nathaniel about her plan to save the world with a Skid Row salvage company, and Nathaniel filled her in on the importance of music in his life.

"My favorite piece is Beethoven's Sixth," says Carol, who, at first glance, looks like she got lost on the way to high tea and ended up on Skid Row. She's neatly dressed and coiffed, a white woman in her mid-seventies in a population dominated by young black males.

"The Pastorale," Nathaniel says, breaking from his music to eavesdrop. Then he raises his right hand to conduct the Sixth.

At the moment, I'm more interested in Carol than in Nathaniel. What's her story, and what can it tell me about a disease I know so little about? Carol is happy to oblige. Forty years ago, she was a homemaker in the Highland Park neighborhood north of downtown Los Angeles. She and her husband, a floral designer, had two children, and all was good until Carol began feeling an uncontrollable, feral urge to run through the streets at night. She slept in neighbors' yards and on the street while her husband searched hysterically for her, often with the two children riding lookout in the family car. He would find her, take her back home, and she'd run again, eventually landing in a mental hospital, where she picked a fight with the first person she saw.

"I'm different," Carol tells me. "I'll admit to a lot of anger in me. And paranoia, too. It's not so much fear as it is suspicion."

She says she thought her husband was trying to poison her and that there was something sinister about the television set in their home.

"I was getting messages from the TV," she says.

What kind of messages?

Carol levels her eyes at me and arches her brow.

"That's personal, Steve," she says sternly.

I back off, apologizing, but Carol proceeds, moving from the conspiracy of TV transmissions to the voices that fill her head. It's not clear why she's offended by a question about the TV but comfortable describing the ghosts who trespass at will, but I'm happy to take what I can get.

"It's never anything like, 'Go kill yourself.' It's just someone calling my name. I don't know who it is, but it's happened four times in the last six months."

I ask her if she thinks medication might help quell those voices.

Last time she tried meds, Carol tells me, her legs turned to jelly and she was in a fog for days. There's nothing she loves more than cracking open a good book, but the drugs make it impossible.

When she's not reading, Carol says, she's gathering up bottles and cans across Skid Row and taking them to a redemption center. The world wastes too much, and she has been called upon to one day operate a recycling operation of unprecedented size. I wonder if she thinks she might be limited by age or the fact that she's living at a mental health shelter.

"I've got to dream," she says.

Mollie Lowery, who established Lamp in 1985, retired at about the time I met Nathaniel. Though I didn't know her well, it was comforting to have her offer occasional words of encouragement as she followed Nathaniel's story in the newspaper. Lowery is a lanky native Angeleno with a saint's heart and an activist's soul, who moved from one cause to another as a young woman, looking for something important to devote herself to. In the 1970s, while working with homeless people at the Ocean Park Community Center in West Los Angeles, she noticed a sudden explosion of mentally ill people wandering the streets. The state hospitals had been closed and patients were told to go home, but many of them had no homes to return to. As for the limited mental health services that did exist, there was one problem. Untreated mentally ill people do not by nature rise and shine each morning and go queue up at the nearest county health office. The people in the greatest need of help, Lowery realized, were not about to fill out forms, keep appointments or trust anyone remotely associated with a mental health service, particularly since many of them had endured mind-boggling bureaucracy or had been force-fed medication that made them feel like slugs.

Lowery, on a fact-finding mission, traveled fifteen miles east, from beach to skyscrapers, to see if the Skid Row missions and other service centers had figured out what to do about any of this. What she found was that if Santa Monica had a growing problem, Skid Row had a full-blown epidemic. Mentally ill people by the hundreds were roaming the streets, and by night they became part of a box city asylum, with cardboard from the toy, flower and garment districts serving as sidewalk homes. It was the ground zero of failed public policy. Only one place, the Downtown Women's Center, seemed to have any idea what to do about the problem. It offered basic services like food and shelter before trying to impose treatment, and the loose structure appeared to be drawing women in from the cold.

Lowery became convinced that was the way to go—to build a welcoming place without judgment, a place where clients could be themselves in a setting without expectation or rigid rules. In her search for a way to create such a shelter, she met a man named Frank Rice, whose politics could not have been more unlike hers. He was a chamber of commerce conservative and vice president of Bullock's department store, but Rice was no less compassionate than Lowery and at least as determined to serve the needy and clean up downtown in the process. Rice suggested Lowery open a center for men, since there was no place for them at the Downtown Women's Center, and he had the muscle to get city officials moving and cash flowing. The result was the Los Angeles Men's Project.

I wasn't living in Los Angeles at the time and knew nothing of Lowery's work. I was living in Philadelphia, where, by chance, Sister Mary Scullion was doing the same thing. Whereas politicians and public policy designers had failed, and while most of us were inclined to do little more than grumble about the unsightly presence of panhandlers and bums, Scullion took her vow of humility into the streets on the most bitter nights of many a Philadelphia winter, determined to reel in those who had been cut loose. I heard about Scullion from a *Philadelphia Inquirer* reporter named Vernon Loeb, who had a suggestion one year when I asked if he had any ideas for an upbeat Thanksgiving Day column.

"Go see Sister Mary," Loeb said.

"What's she do?" I asked.

"She goes out on the street and talks to mentally ill homeless women."

"And that's an upbeat Thanksgiving story?"

"She gets them to come live in some old abandoned school," Loeb said. "Go check it out. If you don't feel inspired by the hope in there, I'll buy you lunch."

He never bought that lunch.

Scullion had taken the name of her order, Sisters of Mercy, to heart. A couple of dozen women were living at her shelter, and she introduced me to them as if they were members of her family. They were sick and hobbled and showed the scars and strain of too many years outside, but in the eyes of each, there were the signs of recovered confidence, dignity and hope. They were trying to find some balance, hooking up with long-lost relatives and getting used to the idea of pitching in to make this new place their home.

While Scullion focused first on women and later branched out to include men, Lowery was doing it in reverse out west. Both were being recognized as pioneers, and neither was very comfortable taking bows. They were quick to tell their admirers that the real heroes were the thousands of desperate, addled, courageous souls who had graced and enriched their lives.

"When you look in Mollie's face, you can see that she has absorbed the grief of the people she treats," an admirer once said of Lowery. "In the business she's in, you can either put up a shield so the unhappiness doesn't touch you, or you can be open to it and absorb it yourself. What makes Mollie so interesting is that she has absorbed it, and—how can I say this?—she has grown strong from it."

Yes, it is exhausting work, Mollie concedes one day when we sit in her backyard, several miles from Skid Row. But, she assures me, there are rewards. "There's some equality in the relationship. A lot of people think social work is just giving, giving, giving, but it's not. There's far more getting. The simple appreciation people had for the smallest things we did for them always amazed me."

People are all around, hectoring, cajoling, arguing with one another and getting a little too close for Nathaniel's comfort, just as he feared. When no one is looking, he sneaks his cello back into its case and makes for the door. A Lamp staffer catches him as he steps clear of the door, moments from a clean break, and pulls him back inside. Nathaniel resists at first but finally gives in, hands back the cello and walks away. Like a pouting child, he stops halfway down the street, angrily removes a tennis ball and a Christmas stocking from his shopping cart, and bounces the ball against the wall, catching it with the stocking.

He stays away from Lamp for three long days, and I wonder

if he's done with the place, as well as with me and my rules. On the day of his return he makes music again in the courtyard, but with a different ending this time. This time, he sneaks off with his new instruments. In my effort to help him, I have succeeded only in further complicating his life. He's out there now with two violins and a cello, inviting a mugging. He, of course, is the challenged one, but in a contest of wit and will, he's winning. It isn't even much of a contest.

6

While Nathaniel was at Juilliard, the rare black student in the elite world of conservatory music, I was at a junior college in the San Francisco Bay Area, where white suburban kids who couldn't crack four-year schools were killing time while avoiding the draft. When a counselor told me San Jose State had a good journalism school, I transferred and graduated two years later, beginning a sportswriting career that didn't last two years.

It quickly occurred to me that ballplayers didn't much care for sportswriters and that I didn't much care for ballplayers. They were coddled and pampered and, worst of all, they were jocks like me and tended to be ignorant of the world. I preferred watching ball games from a distance, where it was easier to suffer illusions about the poetry and grandeur of competition, so I gave up the sports beat and became a news reporter at the *Oakland Tribune.* Every assignment there—murder, mayhem, ribbon cuttings, court-room drama, meetings and more mayhem—was an education.

That was when I became mesmerized by the work of columnists Mike Royko and Jimmy Breslin, admiring them from afar. They were watchdogs, detectives, champions, poets and gods, free to roam Chicago and New York looking for someone to speak up for or to poke in the eye with a stick. They were suspicious of power and pretense, just like my blue-collar parents had always been, and they delighted in cutting phonies down to size. It was the late Bob Maynard, then editor of the *Oakland Tribune*, who turned me loose to give it a whirl. I struggled with my first columns there, just as I did after moving on to the *San Jose Mercury News* and *Philadelphia Inquirer*. It was in Philadelphia in the mid-1980s that I had an epiphany. The challenge isn't to figure out how to write, I realized, but why. Without a mission and a sense of whom you write for, you aren't worth reading.

In March 2005, not long after I met Nathaniel, the publisher of the *Los Angeles Times* was fired. John Puerner called his departure "self-imposed," but I wasn't alone in thinking it looked like one of those deals where you have two options—walk away quietly, or be pushed out a window. His chief crime had been to buck his bosses at the *Chicago Tribune*, who kept pushing for staff reductions to keep the profit margins in the 20 percent range and higher. Puerner had argued that although newspapers were struggling through a revolution, with readers dying off or switching to the Internet, only a fool would think you could cut your way to higher profits. But we were at the mercy of Wall Street, and to that breed, all that matters is cash flow. If today's is a penny less than yesterday's, there's panic in pinstripes, and blowback in newsrooms.

In the *Times* office, I joke with media writer Jim Rainey that instead of having tour groups visit the lobby museum, they should be brought up to the editorial offices to watch us fossilize at our keyboards. We revel in our collective misery, but I also worry about whether my job will exist as long as I need it to. I've got to get a two-year-old from Huggies to high school, and if the rumors can be believed, the editor who hired me could be the next to go. John Carroll is a Southern gentleman whose integrity and high standards have become liabilities. Though he is only sixty-three, he won't hang around if ordered to keep shredding the staff he has built, and I'm asking myself if I'll want to continue working for a company that has no place for John Carroll. I probably owe Nathaniel my gratitude for becoming such a distraction that there's less time to grouse and fret. For all the trouble he's giving me, Nathaniel is still a good story, and a chance for me to prove why the work that we do matters. But if I'm going to try to navigate the mental health system, I'd better find myself a good guide.

We meet at Canter's Deli, a landmark in the Fairfax District of Los Angeles. I know little about Richard Van Horn, an affable cherub with a bald pate, except that he had been an Episcopal priest who segued into mental health more than two decades ago. A *Times* reporter named Jeanne Merl told me Van Horn works in Long Beach, where he is president of the National Mental Health Association of Greater Los Angeles. Maybe, Merl suggested, he can help me figure out what to do about Nathaniel.

For our first get-together, Van Horn brings along his wife,

Kay, a former congressional aide equally steeped in mental health policy. They both know Nathaniel from my column, and by that, I don't mean they know of him. They know him, and countless others just like him, intimately. The Van Horns are caught up in the drama of his struggle, and in my struggle to help him, and they say there's already been a breakthrough. After decades of inadequate services and lack of awareness or compassion, Nathaniel has put a human face on the suffering of thousands and on the work of those, like the Van Horns, whose mission is to help them.

Nathaniel may indeed be a godsend, but I wasn't fishing for compliments. I confess to the Van Horns that I honestly don't know what else I can do to help Nathaniel. I wonder if I've already erred in leading him to Lamp, where the loose structure doesn't appear to be working very well in his case.

Slow down, the Van Horns tell me. I couldn't have done much better than Lamp. It's set up like the Village in Long Beach, where Van Horn makes his office. The Village was one of the models for the Mental Health Services Act, approved by California voters in late 2004, which puts a small tax on the wealthiest Californians. Van Horn says there's now a chance to pay penance for the sin of shutting the state mental hospitals decades earlier and never following up on the promise of community programs to pick up the slack. Skid Row is no accident, he says. We created it. But there will now be more money for, among other things, the very thing I'm attempting to do with Nathaniel—gradually luring people in off the streets and housing them in places with all the necessary supportive services, like counseling and job training.

Hearing this makes me feel a little better, and maybe even

more hopeful. But then Van Horn tells me what I don't want to hear. This work isn't easy or quick. It requires the patience of Job, which means, of course, that I'm the wrong man for the assignment. But if I stick with it, Van Horn says, I can make a meaningful difference in Nathaniel's life. And if I need some inspiration or guidance, he knows someone I should pay a visit to.

The Village is a three-story redbrick building on the corner of Fourth and Elm, a couple of miles from the sprawling port of Long Beach and the *Queen Mary*. I'm directed to a waiting room, where a man sits on a chair with his head tilted back, staring up as if he expects the ceiling to fall. He's munching an apple and wearing what is either a lamp shade or an unusually large straw hat. I walk past him and into a low-ceilinged room with several desks and subterranean windows that look up onto the street. Dr. Mark Ragins is behind his desk in a corner, talking on the phone. He's practically all hair from the neck up, a Deadhead character with a voice that comes up from his chest. He finishes the call and asks what exactly I've come to talk about.

When I tell him I'm trying to figure out what to do about Nathaniel, he asks how long I can wait because a walk-in patient has just arrived. Would Ragins let me sit in on their session? I ask. He thinks it over for a moment and says sure, and it's an early signal that Ragins has decided to forget everything he learned in medical school.

The walk-in patient turns out to be the man with the lamp

shade. He's wearing baggy gym shorts and black boots, and around his neck he has tied a black shirt, a white towel and a red kerchief, the kind of neck gear Nathaniel often wears. He keeps his head tilted back when he sits down, and I realize it might be to keep his dark shades in place, because the earpieces are gone.

Ragins asks his name.

David.

"You have a very strange appearance," Ragins says.

David doesn't appear to be insulted.

"I do what I can," he says.

"Well," Ragins says, "how can we be of help to you?"

I'm dying for a diagnosis. Is this guy schizophrenic? Does he have what Nathaniel's got? But a diagnosis isn't of much interest to Ragins. Diagnosis, prescription. That's the history of mental health treatment, and Ragins believes it has been a colossal failure. As he sees it, we're not even really sure what labels like schizophrenia and bipolar disorder mean, nor do we have very strong evidence that medication is the best response. That doesn't mean that in the case of someone who is acutely psychotic, and a threat to himself or someone else, Ragins would argue against meds and hospital care. But he's seen far too many people like David avoid seeking help for fear of being thrown into a loony bin against their will. To him, the first order of business is to establish the makings of a relationship that extends beyond the illness. It starts with making a person comfortable to come in on his own, rather than in a straitjacket. David is here today because a Village employee has already made several contacts with him, building up enough trust to finally get him through the door.

David tells Ragins he's been staying at a Skid Row hotel he absolutely hates. It's too hot and swarming with drug dealers, pigeons and insects. He has to wear this hat for protection. And by the way, his foot hurts, he can't hold a job and he needs to figure out how to find another place to live.

"I've had, like, schizophrenia," he says without being asked, telling Ragins he has been on antipsychotic medication in the past, including while living in San Francisco.

"Do you find reasons to move all the time?" Ragins asks.

No, David says. He left San Francisco because his girlfriend was a heroin addict.

"I was with her for way too long."

"Were you in love with her?" Ragins asks.

"I think that's what they call it," David says. "I was stupid."

"Maybe being stupid and being in love are the same thing," Ragins says.

"You tell me, doctor."

Having loosened him up, Ragins does a little digging now, finding that David has sought help in the past and is in a tailspin of late.

"I'm very depressed," he says, and he thought about killing himself while living in San Francisco. "I've been to the bridge, but never jumped."

Ragins asks why not.

"I'd still like to live."

In less than thirty minutes, Ragins has steered him into talking about a set of goals. The doctor asks about his interests, hobbies, desires, establishing in concrete ways that David has a life worth living. David says he's been studying Chinese because it "opens my mind," and he'd like to find a job and a girlfriend.

I suggest that he kill two birds with one stone by finding himself a Chinese girlfriend, and David kind of likes the idea.

"Do you think the way you dress will scare off women?" Ragins asks.

"Maybe the gold diggers," David quips.

Ragins tells David he can get him into a nearby hotel room that will be covered by his disability check. He also gives him a referral to a foot doctor and asks David if he needs medication for depression or the voices he hears. David says he's okay for now, but he'd like to return soon for another chat.

When David leaves I tell Ragins everything I know about Nathaniel and wonder if it sounds like the same kind of schizophrenia David has. Ragins gets a chuckle out of the question. I'm the student who has missed the whole point of the lesson. Making a diagnosis isn't as important as making a connection, Ragins says. If Nathaniel is going to get better, it won't be because of a correct diagnosis and textbook treatment program, but because he develops enough trust in me and others to pursue his own recovery.

There's a reason Ragins's book *A Road to Recovery* isn't called *A Road to a Cure*. There is no cure. But he believes David and Nathaniel can rebuild their lives in a setting like the one at the Village and at Lamp, where they can develop a sense of belonging and learn how to manage the disease. My involvement in Nathaniel's life can make a huge difference for him, Ragins says. He tells me the challenge for doctors, mental health workers and advocates is to treat the person and not the disease.

Before I leave the Village, I ask Ragins if several people who sit near him are also doctors, and the answer is a surprise. No, he says, they're outreach workers who spend much of the day on the street, trying to talk the Davids and Nathaniels in. And they do bring one big advantage to that line of work. All of them once sat in the same chair as David.

7

Every time the phone rings at night, my stomach does a flip. I'm always sure it's the police, calling to say Nathaniel is hanging on by a thread after a mugging, and nice going, Mr. Columnist. Along with giving him two brand-new instruments, why didn't I paint a bull's-eye on his back? When I let Nathaniel know how worried I am about his safety, he tells me to relax, assuring me he has jettisoned enough of his belongings to make room for the new violin and cello on his buggy and keep them covered. "You can't tell what's under all the blankets and other junk," he says.

I argue again that he's broken our agreement to leave them at Lamp, but he says it's just not necessary and insists the instruments will be less secure in someone else's custody. I don't worry about it so much by day, when he plays in relatively safe areas. But I don't know what it's like for him when he retires to Skid Row, and I have my doubts about his ability to safely conceal a three-piece string section.

"Nathaniel," I say to him one afternoon near the tunnel at Second and Hill, "I think I might come spend the night with you one of these evenings."

This gets his attention. He looks at me like I'm the crazy one.

"Why would you do that?"

"Why not? I'd just like to see where you stay and what it's like out there."

He still doesn't understand it, but says if I insist, he's been bedding down on Los Angeles Street near Winston.

"It's in the Toy District," he says, meaning an area where dozens of merchants sell wholesale toys that arrive by ship from across the Pacific. At night, the corrugated doors of those shops are rolled down and padlocked, and the huddled masses take up residence on sidewalks. "Los Angeles is a Beethoven city, but you have Walt Disney, Colonel Sanders, LAPD, the blacks, all the Yo-Yo Ma people, Jews, like JEW-liard, homosexuals. They've got one, two, three homosexual bars down there. The Toy District. That's where all the children get their nourishment. You look up and see the banners that say 'Toy District,' with all the children flying over rooftops."

The longer I'm with him, the more I hear a preoccupation with race, ethnicity and sexual preference. This is not uncommon, a Lamp staffer has told me. With schizophrenia, there's often bigotry or hyper-religiosity, or both. I wonder if Nathaniel's take on race has something to do with having left an all-black neighborhood in Cleveland and ending up in an elite New York school where blacks were scarce. His social development essentially stalled with his breakdown, which came at a time when race in America was a raw, divisive subject. At Second and Hill, I've seen him draw swastikas on the pavement and call fellow African-Americans niggers. He has told me he's brown, not black, pointing to his skin as if the color should be obvious to me.

"I'll be out there tonight," I tell him.

"You don't want to go out there," he says.

Does he have something to hide? Or is it a matter of pride, with him not wanting me to see him sleep on the sidewalk?

"I'll see you in the Toy District when it gets dark," I say.

He nods suspiciously. As I walk away from the Little Walt Disney Concert Hall, he's playing "It's a Small World After All."

A modest renaissance is under way, with long-abandoned buildings coming to life, but much of the east side of downtown is still a job center by day and a shadowy memory by night. At Fourth and Main I hit the border of civilization. Pete's Cafe is there, along with a few gentrified apartment buildings, the homes of artists and young urban pioneers. There's a whiff of order and hope. But take one step north, south or east, and the deal is off. At Fourth and Los Angeles, a man lurks in a doorway with product for sale, and he's got his antenna up to make me as customer or cop. I haven't shaved and I'm wearing jeans, sneakers and a ball cap, a getup I think might help me blend in, but in truth I stand out like a tourist in Amish Country. You can't look at anyone here. It's a giveaway. You light the crack pipe, hire the hooker or get out of Dodge. I'm fooling no one, and suspicious eyes track my every step. On the corner, a Dumpster reeks of rotten food and dead flesh. The daytime bustle of Toy District commerce disappears as darkness and indifference grow. The last drafts of sunbaked urine rise off of stained asphalt and concrete. All systems are down and the place smells of doom.

This is where Nathaniel lives, and I need to ask him why. It would be safer to spend his nights where he spends his days. I keep moving and see a prostitute young enough to still be in high school. She's blond and petite, a little angel of a crack whore, swinging along between blow jobs and hits on the pipe.

"Hey, baby," calls a man in a cardboard box.

"How you doing tonight, honey?" she sings back.

The streets are trashed. Drunks are down and out, like fallen soldiers. Nathaniel has been telling me about a beating victim here, and I don't know if he's talking about the unsolved murder I heard about, a case so fresh the body's still in the morgue. Should have seen the guy's face, he said. "I don't know why you beat a person like that."

An unpaid debt. A psychotic blitz. A random blow. Out here, it could have been anything.

I make my way up Winston toward Main and feel as though I could be next. A guy is coming toward me with purpose. I toss a glance over my shoulder to see if he's got company for an ambush. Am I being too paranoid? I'd make an easy mark for a quick mugging. But there's nothing behind me except my shadow. Still, my flesh rises as the man slides by like a shark. A dealer, I guess. Just checking me out and sending a signal that no browsing is allowed. If I'm not buying, it's time to leave the store.

Back on Los Angeles Street, a San Fernando Valley ministry

arrives with a van and a truck and sets up a sidewalk food line, the missionaries chattering in Spanish as they hand out plates of chicken and beans to a growing line of takers. The hungry drop-outs dig in, cleaning bones to a shine and wiping their mouths with the backs of grimy hands. One stumbling Latino drunk begins blubbering after his meal and the missionaries gather around him as he kneels on the pavement. They reach for my hand and take me into the prayer circle. The group leader lays hands on the kneeling drunk, whose tears splatter the pavement, and they all begin to pray in Spanish.

This is the second largest city in the United States. I am three blocks from the Times Building, four blocks from City Hall, out of sight and beyond the collective consciousness. Nothing here exists. The brilliant night skyline, a profit-chart etching, reaches the stars. A woman in distress zigzags toward me. She looks like she might be sixty-five but as she gets closer she's fifty-five, now forty-five, now in her thirties. A young face is cracked, sunburned and coked out. Her hands are filthy, her sweatpants stained in the seat. She circles, wobbles and stumbles to a pay phone and dials. Not two minutes later a siren cuts toward us in surround sound, the piercing wail bouncing off buildings as the four-man engine crew responds to another call in the 911 drama that plays all night every night.

"It's my heart," the woman tells the rescue crew, and they load her up and shuttle her off to County-USC Medical Center as a firefighter/paramedic tells me it never stops. ODs. Beatings. Heart attacks. Bodies laid out in tents and behind Dumpsters. War veterans fallen from wheelchairs and into the fetid streets.

I walk up Winston but turn back when I find myself isolated

one more time with a man emerging from shadows. He's probably just another dealer looking for a sale, but the sound of the siren and the memory of Nathaniel's story of a beating victim are too fresh, so I turn back and linger at the corner, where a bearded man of about sixty is setting down his sidewalk bedding. I ask if he's familiar with the guy who lugs a shopping cart to this street and sleeps here every night.

"Lots of shopping carts out here," he says.

I'm trying to talk him into a bed at Lamp, I tell the guy.

"If he's got a cart," he tells me, sharing a bit of street wisdom that seems obvious now that he mentions it, "that's not the type that's ready to come in."

And why isn't this guy ready to come in? I wonder. He's got no cart. Maybe he's one of the many who can't tolerate the rules and close quarters of the shelters. That's part of what Nathaniel is avoiding, too, I'm sure. But I'm not trying to get him to a shelter, where hundreds of people sack out on cots. If he gets housing through Lamp, it'll be his own place. And if all he wants to do is play music, wouldn't it be easier if he had a safe and quiet home to call his own?

Finally, around nine o'clock, I see the familiar image at the top of Winston, a shadowy figure with a cart in tow. Nathaniel has arrived. He stops under an apartment building with the sonic blast of a rock band pouring through the windows.

"You like the music?" I ask.

"You call that music?" he quips.

He seems happy to see me, given his recommendation that I stay away. He tells me he stopped and bought a chicken dinner at one of the divey little eateries nearby. When he doesn't take his meals at one of the missions, he always has a few bucks in his violin or cello case at the end of a day, even though he doesn't ask for money. The way he lives, it doesn't take much.

He's exhausted, eyes half-mast, body sagging. The cart must feel like it weighs half a ton, and getting it up and down curbs is both a physical workout and a mental strain. Two dead palm fronds rise from the front corners of his cart, as if he's landscaped his mobile home. Two sticks, four feet in length, are crisscrossed at the other end of the basket and wedged through the slots in a Ford hubcap. With a black marker he has written Brahms on one stick, and on the other, Beethoven. He lugs this heap up one last curb and onto the sidewalk, dragging it to his resting place in front of a locked-down storefront. This is where the woman with the soiled pants called 911, and where the missionaries served chicken. A wing bone and a leg are in the gutter and there's a lingering hint of grease in the air.

Why this spot? I ask.

"I know these guys," Nathaniel says of the colony of fellow travelers, none of whom return his glance.

He points toward LAPD headquarters four blocks away. If a fight breaks out and things get nasty, he says, he knows who to count on, who to avoid and where to run. But if he's hemmed in, he has a sawed-off wooden leg of a chair concealed under the sweatshirt tied around his waist. The club is fastened to his belt with a hook fashioned from wire. And, he tells me, he's got the hubcap as a shield. I feel like I'm interviewing a Roman gladiator.

Nathaniel lashes his cart to a padlock on the storefront shutter and begins unpacking for the night. As I watch, I wonder how best to steer us into a conversation about the advantages of sleeping indoors, and that's when I notice the lighted rooms of nearby flophouses and cheapo apartments.

"Wouldn't it be nice to have one of those places up there?" I ask. "It has to be much more comfortable to have a place of your own."

Not interested, Nathaniel says. This is his turf, and he's not leaving.

"I'd rather die where I know my way around. I'm out here breathing fresh air, and I'm not trapped in some apartment, cooped up and unheard of."

Okay, where's Dr. Ragins when I need him? I'd like to hear him respond. But as always with Nathaniel, I'm pretty much on my own. He's a very smart guy, I tell myself, so let's try logic.

"Do you think it makes any sense to stay here if you're trying to get back in shape as a musician?" I ask, thinking I've surely stumped him. "You'd have much more time to practice if you didn't have to pack and unpack your things every day."

He's got an answer. Always an answer.

"My vision—I hate to admit it—but I'm going to have to do what Mozart did, and die. My vision is to stay in good with God and not worry about far-off stuff, just get across the street safely and be thankful. Honor thy mother and father, don't be disrespectful to people, be good and maybe the music will take care of itself."

Journalism school, several thousand columns and a pretty good street education have not prepared me for this. I never expected to be intellectually challenged at every turn, but the guy's living by his wits and I don't have an answer for him. He's got a philosophical take that actually makes sense in a daffy and delusional way, and it's almost as if he's stolen my questions beforehand and is now toying with me.

Since he brought up God, I ask what that means to him. Maybe I can turn it around and suggest that God wouldn't want him to waste all his talent.

"My god doesn't have a name," he says. "Beethoven could be my god."

Okay, I give up for now.

Nathaniel dips into his cart for a list of sheet music. He says he spent some time at the Central Library earlier in the day but couldn't find the desired Brahms double concerto, Tchaikovsky's Variations on a Rococo Theme, Mendelssohn's Third and Fourth Symphonies, Sibelius's Symphony No. 2, and Strauss's *Don Quixote*. He did, however, dig up and copy Camille Saint-Saëns's Concerto for Violoncello. "There's something like eighteen or nineteen notes in a single pickup," he says. "It's very pleasing that Saint-Saëns had all those ideas and was fast enough to get this all down."

Nathaniel goes digging for a whisk broom from his cart and knows exactly where to find it. Dr. Ragins explained that a schizophrenic's mind is cluttered, with images and thoughts strewn everywhere. You can't organize your mind, but you can organize your shopping cart. So you do.

Nathaniel sweeps the sidewalk with maniacal diligence, flicking dead cockroaches and cigarette butts into the gutter to clear a space for his bedding.

"Have to get all this nasty business out of here," he says good-naturedly before turning to me when the job is done.

"Welcome to my humble abode," he says.

There's not much gibberish tonight. No stream of non se-quiturs and jangled prose. But that only makes me more con-fused and frustrated by the mysteries of mental illness. If he can hold it together like this, coming across as a nimble conver-sationalist, why can't he see the madness of bedding down with cockroaches?

He sets a layer of cardboard on the sidewalk, and on top of that a soiled blanket, a sweater, a canvas sheet and then a sleeping bag. From the bowels of the cart he brings up a can of Shasta Tiki Punch soda and offers it to me.

"Care for a drink?"

Hanging off the cart is a broken clock. He has rubber-banded a plastic fork and spoon onto the clock as hands, with the time set at 3 P.M., and he has written my name in the center of the clock.

Just out of curiosity, I ask, what is my name doing on the clock?

"You work for the *Times*," he says, "and this is a timepiece."

To my relief, he wasn't kidding about the way he manages to hide the instruments. I bought him a hard case for the cello, and it's wrapped in blankets on the bottom shelf of the cart. But when he pulls it out and opens the case, it's empty.

"What happened to the cello?" I ask, thinking it's already been stolen.

Nathaniel is smiling as he pulls a blue nylon bag out of the cart. The cello is inside, and the hard case is a decoy.

Nathaniel throws a glance up and down the street. Two dozen people are setting up camp, but no one seems to be looking our way. A man just ten feet away is slumped against the wall, lighting a crack pipe. Nathaniel sets the cello on the sidewalk against the wall, then puts one of his encased violins on top of it before covering both with several layers of blankets and a blue tarp.

"Gotta protect those guys," he says, shaping the covers so that all anyone can see is what looks like a mound of rags.

His original violin, the one from Motter's Music House in Cleveland, goes on the ground next to the shopping cart.

"I use it as my pillow," he says, so there's no way anyone can grab it without his knowing it.

Nathaniel lowers himself onto his sleeping bag and reaches for the Brahms and Beethoven sticks. I assume they're to poke at anyone who comes snooping around, but he says no.

"When the rodents come," he says, pointing the Beethoven stick at the sewer grate, "this guy takes care of them."

Does he beat the rats with the sticks?

"No. You tap it on the ground like this." *Tap, tap, tap.* "It scares them away."

He's a classical musician who has taken a great fall and now finds himself fending off sewer rats, but when I look into his eyes, I find no hint of regret, no recognition of this nightly collision between beautiful thoughts and ugly reality. He is but a man surviving another night by whatever means necessary, without lament. Humbled and exasperated, I ask how he expects to be able to chase rats away with Brahms and Beethoven sticks while he's dead asleep, but he doesn't answer. His miraculous and mixed-up mind is traveling back through time, wrapped around a memory of his brief acting career in high school. He steps up, stands at the edge of the sidewalk like an actor at center stage, and recites *Hamlet* in a Shakespearean accent.

"To be, or not to be, that is the question:
Whether 'tis nobler in the mind to suffer
The slings and arrows of outrageous fortune,
Or to take arms against a sea of troubles,
And by opposing end them? To die, to sleep,
No more, and by a sleep to say we end
The heartache, and the thousand natural shocks
That flesh is heir to. 'Tis a consummation
Devoutly to be wished. To die, to sleep;
To sleep—perchance to dream—ay, there's the rub;
For in that sleep of death what dreams may come,
When we have shuffled off this mortal coil,
Must give us pause. There's the respect
That makes calamity of so long life."

He takes a modest bow before unappreciative Skid Row Theater audience members, most of whom, like Nathaniel, are in their own worlds. A human howl rises in the invisible distance, one of the mad cries that crack the silence now and then on Skid Row. A barefoot and crazed man shakes and shimmies nearby, his skin crawling with bugs. Two salvagers stride by, jangling their sacks of aluminum cans. Nathaniel bows his head and recites the Lord's Prayer—"deliver us from evil"—then opens his eyes to see two prostitutes trespassing on his prayers.

"I think these children of God are going to be okay," he says. "They're going to sleep and dream, like human beings do."

He slides into his sleeping bag and, as if on cue, a rat comes up from the storm drain and scurries toward us. Nathaniel reaches for the Beethoven stick, taps, and the rat retreats.

"Do you think of writers often?" Nathaniel asks. "Do you think of writers the way I think of musicians?"

Yes, I say. I think about great writers and the source of their creative inspiration. Does it spring from knowledge, experience, love, loss?

Nathaniel looks into lighted windows and says he can almost see the masters at work.

"I love to think about musicians," he says. "I can imagine Mozart or Beethoven sitting in a room up there with the light on. They hunger and thirst like we do. It's angelic."

It's after midnight. Nathaniel offers me his dairy crate and a blanket, suggesting that I recline against his mound of possessions and close my eyes.

"I hope you rest well, Mr. Lopez," he says. "I hope the whole world rests well."

I try to sleep but can't. I'm thinking about the rat that came up from the drain. Then, when finally I begin to doze, I hear a siren, or footsteps, or a hacking cough. I spy the pavement for cockroaches. Restless, I walk Skid Row for ninety minutes, past hundreds of campers. They're in doorways and boxes, slumped over in wheelchairs. I'm angry about billions spent in Iraq while bomb-rattled vets live like animals on Skid Row. I'm ashamed that in a region of unprecedented wealth, the destitute and the sick have been shoved into this human corral. I'm frustrated by my inability to do more for Nathaniel. If I can't help him, how can I help any of the others?

When I get back to Nathaniel, he's snoring. I try to join him, but now I'm even more wired. I walk to a hotel and check in, fall onto a bed in my clothes and stare at the ceiling. Nathaniel has gotten to me. In thirty years of rummaging through cities for characters, I've never met one as beguiling or maddening. No, Mr. Ayers, the world is not resting well. I get up, throw cold water on my face and check out of the hotel two hours after arriving. Nathaniel hasn't moved. I tour Skid Row again and it's as spooky as before, and I wonder how to put this into words.

———⚹———

8

Joseph Russo grew up in the upper-middle-class bedroom community of Manhasset on the north shore of Long Island, the son of a school district administrator and a first-grade schoolteacher. His father was an amateur jazz pianist, so Russo's ear was tuned from an early age, but it wasn't until he got both the measles and the mumps simultaneously, in third grade, that he discovered classical music.

"I was out of school for a month, and my teacher sent home some Beethoven albums and a bust of Beethoven, and she said maybe I'd like listening to this while I was recuperating."

Russo fell in love. He decided, while under the weather and still in pajamas, that he would one day play classical music. And so began the piano lessons, which continued until he attended Manhasset High School, whose orchestra didn't have a piano. The teacher asked Russo to pick another instrument, and he chose violin. But the following week, when instruments were handed out, the teacher assigned him a bass.

"We've got plenty of violin players, but no bass player," said his teacher, and Russo never regretted it.

He progressed so quickly, the teacher advised him to take private lessons from a student of the acclaimed Homer Mensch, who was living in Flushing, New York, at the time. Russo again progressed so quickly that his teacher handed him over to Mensch himself, who told Russo he ought to apply to Juilliard.

"Juilliard?" Russo asked. He was looking at Oberlin and Indiana University, but didn't consider himself good enough to break into Juilliard. Mensch convinced him to audition, though, and Russo was more than adequate. Juilliard gave him a partial scholarship, and he began commuting by train in the fall of 1971.

Like many new students, Russo was initially overwhelmed by the intense atmosphere, the demands on students and the talent of the competition. Juilliard was a full-time challenge from eight in the morning until eight at night, when he went back to Penn Station and took the train home, only to practice until bedtime. On the fourth floor at Juilliard, Russo was intimidated by the quality of the music emanating from the little pressure cookers where students practiced between classes. He wondered, still, if he belonged at Juilliard.

One day, while walking to a class on the third floor, he heard a gorgeous and familiar sound from behind the door of a classroom. Having spent years under Homer Mensch's wing, he recognized the sound as that of his mentor, and he decided to steal just a minute or two to peek in and watch the master at work.

"But when I opened the door, it wasn't Mr. Mensch. It was Nathaniel."

Russo was in awe of his classmate, so much so that he was willing to overlook what at times was an abrasive personality. It was September 1971, after all. The riots at Attica State Prison in upstate New York served as a potent and deadly reminder of racial divisions that ran deep and wide in American culture. An all-white guard unit had boasted of bashing inmates with batons they called nigger sticks. So Nathaniel had an attitude? Russo, for one, wasn't surprised. Nathaniel was a young black man trying to prove himself in a mostly white world. And besides, who at Juilliard didn't have problems with the intense pressure from teachers and competition from classmates? Emotional instability was common. Some turned to drugs, retreating to the not-so-secret lair called Stairway E, which spiraled through the center of campus and was often filled with clouds of reefer. All you had to do was open the stairwell door on the third floor, and without leaving the building, you could get a contact high. It was the early seventies, and drugs were everywhere. Nathaniel was no addict, but like others, he wasn't about to wave off whatever was passed down the line when students sneaked into the stairwell. With a quick tug on a joint, self-confidence won a round in the endless battle with self-doubt. For a brief instant, the mind-fuck disappeared into a yellow cloud, and students emerged with glassy-eyed smiles, better equipped to handle the pressure and politics, the swollen egos and even grander insecurities.

Russo walked into the cafeteria one day and into the middle of a conversation about a stunningly good violinist.

"Hey, you hear what happened to Rabin?"

No, what happened?

"He killed himself."

That was Juilliard. The pressure could shore up your belief in yourself. Or, says Russo, "It could destroy you."

His first year at Juilliard, Russo invited some classmates home to Manhasset for a Christmas party. By then, Nathaniel was closer to Russo than anyone else. He appreciated Russo's low-key manner and quick humor, and Russo was struck by Nathaniel's talent and intelligence. They caught a train at Penn Station and rolled out to the burbs with other pals, and as the party got going, several of them gathered around the piano to watch a classmate play. The Juilliard pressure was gone, the spirit was light, the mood festive. And when the pianist finished his piece, Russo turned to Nathaniel.

"Boy," he said, "doesn't that sound beautiful?"

Nathaniel glared back at Russo and the party sounds gave way to silence.

"What do you mean by saying 'boy'?" he demanded.

Russo was dumbstruck at first, then frightened by the change that had come over his friend. It was as if another person had crawled into his skin. Russo had seen sudden mood changes in Nathaniel, but nothing quite like this. He stammered a clarification, saying he hadn't called him a boy. Didn't Nathaniel understand that?

"Are you a racist?" Nathaniel insisted, stopping the party dead. It was a moment so awkward and thick, no one knew what to say or do. Russo was hurt by the accusation. Hadn't he stuck with Nathaniel while others dismissed him as an angry flake? Hadn't he invited Nathaniel into his home to share the holiday with his family? Russo wondered, for the first time, if there might be something seriously wrong with his friend. Finally, someone had the sense to break the tension by starting another piece on the piano. The party resumed, and Nathaniel quickly swung back to normal, drifting with the music and carrying on as if nothing had happened.

9

Although I feel closer to Nathaniel since the night on Skid Row and more determined to help him, it's not clear to either of us what my role is in his life, and I don't know if I've earned the right to tell him he needs psychiatric help. I do know from his sister Jennifer that medication is a sore subject, not just because he insists he doesn't need it, but because he recoils at the mere suggestion of something or someone controlling him. Besides, I assume he'd cleverly deflect the subject, same as he did when I suggested it would make more sense for him to live indoors. But when he seems to be in good spirits one day on Skid Row, I ask if he recalls anything about the treatment he had in Cleveland.

"Woodruff is the first time I'd ever seen shock treatment," he volunteers, referring to a mental hospital his mother had taken him to after he left Juilliard.

Why'd they do it? I ask.

"I guess they don't like quitters."

"Quitters? You got sick."

"I'd quit Juilliard, so they gave me shock treatment," he says. "They give you sodium pentathol. I remember they strap you down so when you come to you don't fall off the table. I would go into a stupor, I guess. I could not understand what was going on in New York at Juilliard. Too many cigarettes. Russians, English, Argentinians, Puerto Ricans. You name it, they were there. I was in the same orchestra as Yo-Yo Ma. I couldn't understand what the constant attack from people was all about."

"What do you mean by that? Who was attacking you?"

"Everybody. A person smoking a cigarette right in front of you. Then I had the pressure of my lessons—to get things prepared. I was all alone, no family, none of my people."

"Which people?"

"The black people."

At times, he says, the medication seemed to help. Thorazine, Haldol, Prolixin, Stelazine. He took all those and more while being treated in Cleveland.

"Any psychotropic drugs will calm you down. Schizophrenia is a disorder in which you don't seem to be able to function as well as you can. My mind would not strive to do all that it could do to keep me lean and interested in staying healthy. My mind would not strive to be the best citizen I could be. My mind would not strive to do what's best for Nathaniel. You have no idea what's going on with God, country, yourself. Your relationship with your family erodes, you have no friends, no human desire. You get into fights."

And you hear voices?

"I don't know if I hear voices or not. I don't know if what I'm hearing is abnormal or not. I think there's an incredible amount of subconscious energy. It emits itself through the brain and into your nervous system."

So would he consider medication again?

Maybe, he says. One day.

A few days later I hand Nathaniel a notepad and ask him to write down some thoughts on his first awareness that something was wrong, and what it was like to be treated for schizophrenia. No rush, I say. Take as much time as you like. A week later he hands back the notepad.

> *As a youngster it was very untogether to be labeled mentally ill because of a underlying cigarette habit. That was the root of all evil. I quit and now I feel well enough.*
>
> *Drug—Abuse*
>
> *Resistance—Education*
>
> *D.A.R.E.*
>
> *The treatments for mentally ill persons is from horrible to okay. Overall the idea of deprivation was very effective—making users of drugs realize that there is a real war against drugs being fought every day in LA—LAPD—DARE 911.*
>
> *Los Angeles, California. Recently there was a stabbing incident near the doorway at Lamp 627 San Julian Street. Black man. Mr. Nathaniel McDowell. Los Angeles Times Steve Lopez LAPD 911 Vice Homicide Narcotics. USMC. USN. USA. USAF. USCG. George W. Bush. Command N. Chief of United States Armed Forces.*
>
> *L.A. Psychiatric. Psychiatrist Dr. Eduardo D. Vasquez, MD.*
>
> *In the state of California—murder = a crime of a much more serious nature than that of a misdemeanor. The penalty for murder is*

death. Death by injection. Governor Arnold Schwarzenegger. Mayor
Antonio Villaraigosa. House Representative Senate Representative.

The Cleveland Browns Art Modell Owner Bernie Kozar Quarter-
back #19.

The Denver Broncos Jerry Boland Owner. John Elway Quarter-
back #7.

It goes on like that for two more pages, ending with this:

Pens from Steve Lopez
Many thanks.
Paper from Steve Lopez.
Many thanks.
Cello & Violins from Steve Lopez
Many thanks

Among my many new pen pals is Stella March, the mother of a
son with schizophrenia, who is roughly Nathaniel's age. Few people in California have done more than she to enlighten the public and prod lawmakers into reforming a mental health system
that had been a national embarrassment for years. And she's done
almost all of it on a volunteer basis.

March writes me encouraging notes about Nathaniel and my
efforts on his behalf, but seldom offers specific advice, although
she is the one who has taught me Nathaniel is not a mentally ill
musician, as I've been referring to him, but a musician with mental illness. It's a subtle but significant difference, recognizing the
person before the condition. I've been meaning to go talk to her,
and for two reasons, now is the time. First, I find myself haunted

by Nathaniel's long and rambling scribbles, and wonder if she can put them in perspective and suggest strategies I might try. And second, March is the one person in Los Angeles who can best answer the absurd comments about mental illness that have just been made by actor Tom Cruise, of all people.

We meet at a coffee shop in Westwood, near the University of California at Los Angeles. March, a white-haired widow who would have to stand on the Los Angeles phone book to reach five feet, has spent decades trying to undo stereotypes about mental illness, and Cruise has created a stir with his unsolicited comments on the subject. Specifically, Cruise said actress Brooke Shields didn't need medication for postpartum depression. In his opinion, she needed vitamins. There's no such thing as a chemical imbalance, Dr. Cruise argued, appearing on *Access Hollywood* and the *Today* show, basing his expertise on interventions with fellow Scientologists.

"I've never agreed with psychiatry, ever," Cruise told *Today* show host Matt Lauer. "Before I was a Scientologist I never agreed with psychiatry, and when I started studying the history of psychiatry, I understood more and more why I didn't believe in psychology."

March rolls her eyes. Cruise's comments would be laughable, she says, except that he's liable to be believed by many people. I know I'd love to think that with a monthly supply of One-A-Day vitamins, Nathaniel will be performing with the Los Angeles Philharmonic by mid-June. But I have my doubts, and March assures me there's overwhelming evidence and general agreement among doctors and researchers that mental illness results from a chemical imbalance. In the case of schizophrenia, research points to a biological brain disorder involving any number of abnormalities—including irregular function of a neurotransmitter called dopamine—that could create hallucinations and distort reality.

March is the force behind "StigmaBusters," an ever-vigilant service of the National Alliance on Mental Illness. She gathers examples of stereotypes, slights and ill-informed rants to try to educate the offenders and the public. Her plan now is to contact the producers of Cruise's new movie, *War of the Worlds*, and threaten to organize a boycott if there's not an apology.

Cruise has brilliantly bolstered all the primitive thinking about mental illness, making it out to be a choice born of moral and spiritual weakness. Stigma, March says, keeps families from accepting a loved one's illness and seeking treatment for them, and it also marginalizes those who are afflicted. Why else, she asks me, would it be socially acceptable for them to sleep on filthy and dangerous streets? Would anyone tolerate an outdoor dumping ground for victims of cancer, ALS and Parkinson's?

As we sip coffee, I tell March I'd like to give Cruise a tour of Skid Row and see if he thinks a vitamin deficiency explains the mad scene there. I feel like I'm talking to a kindred spirit in March, and our shared experience—though hers has lasted much longer and involves her own flesh and blood—is a source of comfort. I feel so at ease, I decide to tell March I've been thinking lately about two suicides, years ago, in my family.

My aunt Mary's was the first. I remember coming home from school one day in 1963, when I was ten, and being startled to find so many relatives in our living room. My dad's sister, who was married with a daughter in college and a son in high school, had driven down to the river in our small suburb of San Francisco and jumped in. A year later, my dad's brother Manuel, a handsome gent who had a wife and son and enjoyed kidding around with his nieces and nephews, shot himself in the head.

I don't recall the word "suicide" being used in either case. They were sick. That's what I was told. It was a time when depression was often thought of as the blues rather than a treatable medical condition, and in my family, it wouldn't have occurred to anyone to get help for the blues, especially from a shrink.

The suicides were but a distant memory—and seldom talked about in my family—until I met Nathaniel and learned more about mental illness. It tends to run in families, and I worry what that means, if anything, for my two sons and daughter. Not that there's anything to do but be vigilant and take any warning signs seriously. I've been unable to find any evidence of mental illness in the history of Nathaniel's family, and March tells me there was none in hers, either, unless it was there but undiagnosed, as might have been the case with my aunt and uncle. Her son was nineteen when it hit. He was a UCLA history major on the dean's list. One day, without warning, he collapsed on the steps of a campus building.

"They took him to the ER and then the psychiatric emergency ward. After that, it's too . . . it's just been a terrible journey. He was at Camarillo State Hospital, which at that time was just horrible—the most horrible place in the world. It was like a zoo. They gave him thorazine, which I think has had a lot to do with his lack of recovery. That was what they believed in back then, and my husband had gone to all the medical libraries to find out what they knew about how to treat mental illness, and very little was known at the time."

Doing something about it has become her life's work. Today March's son lives in a board and care home, meets regularly with a psychiatrist and takes medication to control his condition. March knows there's still a long way to go for him and for the cause she's still committed to, but she's encouraged by improvements in awareness—Tom Cruise's outburst notwithstanding—and a breakthrough in brain scan technology that could one day allow doctors to diagnose schizophrenia in its early stages.

Maybe that won't do her son much good, March tells me, or Nathaniel, either, for that matter. I do worry, I admit, that Nathaniel might be too far gone to have a breakthrough now, having become so set in his ways after decades without treatment.

March touches my hand and looks me in the eye. She points out that he didn't have a friend before me, and he didn't go to Lamp at all, and no one can predict where it will lead from here. Yes, he's still very sick, she says, but there were times when she didn't think her son would be doing as well as he is.

I appreciate the way she chooses her words. She promises nothing and doesn't try to simplify matters, but she makes me feel as though no matter what happens, I can call her and she'll understand.

10

Alexis Rivera is riding his bicycle to Little Pedro's Blue Bongo from his home in Echo Park when he comes upon a captivating image and hits the brakes. A middle-aged man stands alone at the mouth of the Second Street tunnel playing violin as if he's onstage at Carnegie Hall. This must be the guy he's read about.

Rivera decides to take in the concert. This is an odd place to play, given the constant roar of passing vehicles, but to Rivera that only makes the image all the edgier and more interesting. A helicopter goes by, Disney Hall is just up the hill. For Rivera, something about the scene captures the energy of the city.

Should he introduce himself?

No, Rivera decides. This is real and honest. Just let it be.

But why not? Doesn't this musician deserve to be seen and heard?

Rivera keeps watching, imagining the violinist performing at the Blue Bongo a mile away on First Street, where Rivera is one of the managers. Rivera is intrigued by the idea, but another voice tells him not to exploit the situation. He doesn't want to promote some kind of freak show featuring a homeless violinist who is mentally ill.

But he can't help it. Rivera walks over and introduces himself.

"That sounded great," he says.

Nathaniel isn't one to kick aside a compliment. He's genuinely flattered when people tell him they enjoy his music, and he's clever enough to get his adoring fans to repeat their praise.

Yes, Rivera assures him. It was terrific. Would he consider coming by his club one evening to play a set? There wouldn't be much money in it, maybe ten or twenty bucks plus tips. But his music ought to be heard.

"What?" Nathaniel asks.

Rivera tells him he's not kidding.

"Nobody has asked me to do that in thirty years," Nathaniel says.

He tells Rivera he isn't sharp enough for a gig, and he won't be able to do much about his appearance. Who'd want to go to a club and see some bum walk in off the streets, nappy-haired and raggedy? Besides, he doesn't go anywhere without his shopping cart, and he can't very well wheel it up onstage.

Rivera says that's not a problem.

"How about Tuesday nights?" He tells Nathaniel he'll go on right before Mickey Champion, a blues singer turned public school cafeteria worker whose career Rivera is trying to revive, even though she's old enough to be his grandmother. If Nathaniel gets to the club early enough, Rivera says, he can have dinner on the house.

"If I have dinner before I perform, I'll throw up," Nathaniel tells him.

Rivera takes that as a yes. And Nathaniel, who has already spent several hours practicing, goes back to work with renewed purpose.

She asks to remain anonymous. As a psychiatrist working for the Los Angeles County Mental Health Department, she says it's not her place to engage in a public debate about competing philosophies on how to treat mental illness. But she has e-mailed me to say she had a problem with my column about the Village in Long Beach and the "recovery" model used by Dr. Mark Ragins.

A "warm and fuzzy" embrace won't get the job done, she argues when I call, pooh-poohing the notion that doctors should focus on patients' lives rather than just treating their symptoms. Chronically mentally ill patients are sick, she says, and sometimes dangerously so. They need psychiatric counseling and medication, not sunshine and hugs. She goes on to say she is horrified by the fact that the Village is a model for California's Mental Health Services Act. If that's the direction the state is headed in, she argues, it's going to pour billions of dollars into a bottomless pit while the sick go untreated.

Does she know what she's talking about? As a matter of pride, I'd like to think not, having become a believer in Ragins's program. She's got me wondering, though, whether I naively bought into the idea that Nathaniel could get better with such a passive approach. Then again, he's now visiting Lamp a few times a week for meals and showers. I'd be much happier if he used the place as something other than a pit stop, but maybe it's just a matter of time.

Curiosity, and the need to bang out another column, make for a rare brainstorm. I'll invite Dr. Ragins and the anonymous psychiatrist to meet Nathaniel at Little Pedro's. We can all chat, they can watch him perform and the doctors and I can hash out the best treatment plan after the show.

Unfortunately, my plan doesn't work out. Ragins is out of town and the county psychiatrist is still a little gun-shy. But I don't give up. In Ragins's place I manage to recruit Dr. Vera Prchal, a psychiatrist who occasionally works at Lamp and is a practitioner of the so-called recovery model, and in place of the county psychiatrist I get her boss, Dr. Rod Shaner, medical director of the Los Angeles County Mental Health Department.

Now all I have to do is produce the star of the show.

I pull up around 6:30 with a bad case of nerves, worrying that Nathaniel might not show. Don't sweat it, he said earlier. But I couldn't find him when I left my office, and even if he's on his way, the shopping cart will slow him down. Alexis Rivera, meanwhile, is up in the San Francisco Bay Area with a band he manages, so I guess I'm the fallback promoter for the evening.

Little Pedro's Blue Bongo is a dark and cavernous joint that looks like a Mexican bus station and smells like spilled beer. I find the two doctors inside and we order dinner. Prchal, a svelte woman with blond hair and golden skin, was born and trained in

Czechoslovakia. Shaner, with a shaved head and a runner's body, was chief of the psychiatric emergency room at County-USC Medical Center before a promotion to medical director of the mental health department. Both of them have read about Nathaniel and they're looking forward to meeting him.

I lay out the inspiration for this gathering, telling the doctors that I'm trying to figure out who's right about the most effective way to treat people like Nathaniel. Is it Ragins, or is it the Ragins critic?

Shaner thoughtfully considers my question while picking at his dinner. Then, with an expression that says he knows I won't like the answer, he says: "They're both right."

It's not what I want to hear. I want a clear signal as to how to proceed, so I can quickly pass the responsibility for Nathaniel's welfare over to someone who knows what they're doing. Yes, I like the guy immensely, but I just don't have the time to be his primary caretaker.

Some people need medication to survive, Shaner says. Others don't respond well to a push and would be better served by a Village or Lamp model. There is no right or wrong, and there are no absolutes. Prchal, unfortunately, sees it the same way. She says patients like Nathaniel, who have been forcibly hospitalized or had negative reactions to medication, often aggressively resist any efforts to help them. They don't want to hear about a new generation of antipsychotic meds with fewer side effects because they just don't trust anyone. But no two cases are alike, the doctors tell me, and there is no such thing as a universal model for treating people like Nathaniel. Of course, they'd have to see him to know more, but as the clock strikes seven, he's still a no-show.

I apologize and order another round of drinks, trying to buy some time, but I'm worried the night will be a disaster. I fill the doctors in on everything I know about Nathaniel, but I'm afraid I'm wasting their time and my own as well. Working nights is part of the job, but the chances for a column from Little Pedro's are waning, and all the extra time I'm spending on Nathaniel is time I don't get to spend with my family. I wouldn't mind it so much if I knew I was making a bigger difference in Nathaniel's life, but there's no telling if or when that would ever happen. Meanwhile, I'm hearing about too many little developments in Caroline's life by phone. She's stringing more words together, trying more foods and wondering where I am half the time. Alison, a freelance writer whose schedule is more flexible than mine, supports and appreciates what I'm doing with Nathaniel, but both of us are overwhelmed with busy schedules, and she keeps getting stuck with more of the burdens at home because I routinely break promises to be home earlier.

It's now 7:30 at Little Pedro's. Dinner is done and I'm running out of things to talk about as the doctors check their watches. Finally, at eight, I tell them I'll go look for him if they can hold on just a little longer. I pull out of the Little Pedro's lot and hit the gas, and half a block away I see him coming down the street, the palm fronds sticking up from the shopping cart. The Brahms and Beethoven sticks are crisscrossed through the hubcap, his belongings piled high. It looks like he's got a small elephant on a leash.

"I thought you forgot," I say. "Where have you been?"

He's panting when he pauses to rest.

"I had another engagement," he says.

Scolding him will do no good. Exasperated and relieved, I tell him to hurry, because time is running out.

He agrees to leave the cart with the parking attendant, and this is a first. I carry the cello inside and he takes care of the two violins. I tell him Shaner and Prchal are friends of mine. There's no telling what he might do if I say they're doctors. They say hello, but there's no time for psychoanalysis. Several people have come over from the bar to sit by the stage in anticipation of his performance. Nathaniel barely acknowledges them as he tunes up, and I can't tell whether he's in a bad mood or nervous.

Is this the worst idea I've ever had? In my eagerness to get an appraisal from two psychiatrists, and another column to boot, have I done just what Alexis Rivera intended to avoid? Have I exploited Nathaniel? I wanted to believe that Rivera's recognition of his talent and the offer of a stage would give him new purpose and advance his recovery, but putting a man with mental illness in front of a live audience suddenly seems selfish and cruel. It occurs to me that maybe he likes playing next to a tunnel because of the anonymity it provides, and because the noise drowns out the mistakes.

As the tuning process drags toward 8:30, I walk up and whisper to Nathaniel that it might be time to get things moving, if he's still up for this. He says he's okay and picks up the violin from Motter's, with "Stevie Wonder" scratched into it. I put a reassuring hand on his shoulder and introduce him to his audience.

"This is my friend Nathaniel," I say, struggling to put him at ease while preparing the audience for an unpolished performance. He's been working hard, I say, "to rebuild a music career that goes back many years." I point out that he was trained on string bass and is teaching himself violin and cello.

Nathaniel gives a nervous nod to quiet applause. I take in the spectators as they eyeball his T-shirt scarf, the doodling on his jeans and the untied sneakers. The bottom of the club he keeps hooked to his belt peeks out from under a sweatshirt tied around his waist.

Nathaniel tentatively fingers his way through a Beethoven-like dirge. There's nothing remarkable about the music and he seems to be struggling. As it gets worse, he turns away from the audience ever so slowly, as if he can't bring himself to face the crowd. Shaner has a finger on his chin. Prchal looks morose. I don't know if they're feeling sorry for him or shocked at me for subjecting him, and them, to this. I'm tempted to put a stop to it and usher him away, though that would only make it worse. But I know he shouldn't be here. In a shaky voice, Nathaniel apologizes for not playing better, but the audience is giving him a pass, applauding his effort, and this seems to shore up his confidence a bit. He switches to cello and works on the tuning.

"It's encouraging," Dr. Prchal says, "that he's aware that he isn't playing well." He can distinguish between how he once played and how he's playing now, she reasons. And she makes a point I haven't considered. Maybe he resists treatment because getting better would mean a return to a life he recalls as unbearable. In a conservatory setting, she says, the pressure is immense, and Nathaniel's talent might have been matched only by his fragility. It is possible that the pressure is what caused him to snap.

Nathaniel looks and sounds more comfortable on cello. The

audience becomes more responsive and his confidence grows, and I relax along with him. It's still clear, even to an amateur like me, that he's missing notes, mixing passages from the Bach cello suites with riffs of his own and struggling with pitch. But he has his moments and feels his way through the set, becoming more animated as the sound becomes soulful. He hits a groove, nails a couple of vibratos and closes his eyes in relief, saved by music and cured, once more, by his own hand. Now the applause is real, and I'm clapping harder than anyone, filled with pride.

Shaner says it's tragic and frightening to think of this man or any other spending his nights on dangerous streets. "I'd like to seduce him into treatment, and he needs seduction," says Prchal, but she knows it won't be easy. "People with his IQ, tremendous ambition and achievement don't like to be ordered around. But this man has to be treated. I will try to meet with him and slowly start some dialogue about the possibility of treatment, and slowly also see if he would want to have his own room."

When we go out back to load his cart, Nathaniel apologizes, saying it didn't go well. I tell him he's wrong. There might have been a couple of rough spots, but he turned it around and ended on a roll.

"You really think so?" he asks.

A couple of days later he hands me a note thanking me for writing about his performance. He says he thinks he could "really start progressing much better" if I could get him a copy of the Bach Cello Suites, a music stand and a new A string for the cello.

He signs it:

Your friend, Nathaniel Anthony Ayers

11

Six months after meeting Nathaniel, my bond with him is deeper and so is my desire to get on with my life. I don't have any intention of abandoning the relationship, but I don't have the stamina to serve indefinitely as his keeper, worrying about his safety while trying to be a columnist, husband and father. The Blue Bongo episode fits a pattern that is wearing me out. He frustrates my efforts to help him and has me on the verge of giving up, and then he pulls through at the last minute in a way that gets me even more hooked on him.

But is he really any better off than he was the day I met him?

Somewhat, I suppose. As Stella March told me that day over a cup of coffee, he has someone in his life who cares about him. He has a connection at Lamp if he wants food or safe, familiar surroundings. We've been invited to a rehearsal by the L.A.

Philharmonic—something that never would have happened if I hadn't met him—and he's excited about it.

But the questions people ask me about him are a reminder of how little has been accomplished.

Has he moved inside?

No.

He's not still living on the street and chasing rats with a stick, is he?

Yes.

Is he on medication?

No.

Does he see a psychiatrist?

No. But I think I need to.

Dr. Prchal's first attempt to "seduce" him into treatment is a bust. She spots him on the street one day and suggests he come see her, and Nathaniel tells her to go away. Anyone whose name begins with "doctor" is no one he cares to see. Maybe if I spend more time with him I can be persuasive, but where would I get it?

If two-year-olds are supposed to be terrible, so far Alison and I are lucky. Despite the required backseat vomiting disaster on the way to a short vacation on California's Central Coast, Caroline is easy to travel with and excited about going places. She calls me Daddy-O, has begun to speak in the past tense—"I goed"—and thinks it's just fine to keep singing "Amazing Grace" without knowing all the words. Fortunately I've caught all the big milestones, but the really good stuff is nothing you can write in a journal. It's an expression that only you can see the changes in, it's the emergence of a personality unique to the world, it's the way she comes out of the bath with her hair slicked back and you catch a glimpse of what she might look like when she's older.

One reason we've come to the Central Coast is to see if it's possible to swing a deal on a condo. If we could buy a place and rent it out to cover the mortgage, we'd have a nice little investment and a place to move to in retirement. From Big Sur to San Luis Obispo and Morro Bay, the spectacular California coast is not yet grossly overdeveloped and the climate is ideal. Alison and I both love the water, the pine-scented air and the plunging coastal cliffs, and Caroline is being trained to share our appreciation. But the places we look at are either too expensive or too shabby, or the rent won't cover the monthly mortgage. And in the back of my mind, there's one more issue. If we moved up here and Nathaniel was still in Los Angeles, who would look after him?

The fact that the question occurs tells me something about the way he's gotten to me. Maybe there's a bit of guilt involved. I'm here in one of the most beautiful and inspiring places in the world, and he's in one of the most wretched. The difference between us is luck. I'm a healthy fifty-two-year-old dad whose life has been made new by a two-year-old's discovery of the world, and he's a fifty-four-year-old former phenom whose development was stopped dead more than thirty years ago.

One morning we return from the beach and I turn on my cell phone after a couple of days of peace. A message had been left, the night before, by Alexis Rivera at the Blue Bongo. Nathaniel is losing it onstage, Rivera says. He's going off on the audience, cursing, angry. Rivera doesn't know what to do. Please call as soon as possible.

"Is he all right?" Alison wants to know.

I have no idea, and Rivera doesn't answer when I call. I'm naturally worried but also upset with myself for allowing it to happen. What a fool I was to think that he could handle a job like that in his condition.

Finally I get hold of Rivera and the upshot isn't so bad. It was pretty scary there for a while, he says, but Nathaniel calmed down and left the stage. He went outside and played on the sidewalk for a while, and some of the patrons went out there to watch him.

It's probably best, I tell Rivera, to put Nathaniel's return to the stage on hold for now.

When the long-dreaded announcement is finally made, it's anticlimactic but still feels like a gut shot. John Carroll, the man who hired me, is resigning to avoid one more day of battling the hog butchers in Chicago. Dean Baquet, who came close to walking away with him, has agreed to take over for Carroll on the promise that the company won't rip the place to shreds for the sake of propping up the stock. In the beaten-down newsroom, there's grief that Carroll is leaving, relief that Baquet is staying and a general agreement that the *Tribune* promise to Baquet is worth less than yesterday's newspaper. Should I begin looking for work, or at least try to come up with a Plan B? I probably would if I weren't so busy. But moving out of town would mean leaving Nathaniel on his own, and the number of desirable jobs out there is shrinking fast. I don't know of a better situation than working for the *Times* under Baquet, a Pulitzer prize–winning reporter and former *New York Times* editor who tells us this is no time to act as if our best work is behind us.

As usual, the steady march of breaking news keeps me from dwelling for too long on things that are out of my control. I hear on the radio that two teenagers with baseball bats have gone on a crime spree in downtown Los Angeles, clubbing street people as they lie sleeping.

Police are saying the teens were inspired by a video series called Bumfights, in which promoters pay street people to beat one another, pull teeth with pliers, set their hair on fire and perform other dangerous stunts. Some of the victims are down-and-out Vietnam vets who never got free of the war's reach. In Los Angeles, one of the victims was beaten in a tunnel and is in critical condition, and I'm certain it's Nathaniel. He has switched up his routine and started sleeping in the Second Street tunnel rather than on Skid Row, and I can imagine him being awakened by the two cowardly thugs and getting beaten as he defends his cello and two violins. This is my fault, and I'll never live it down.

He's probably at County-USC Medical Center, but I'm too afraid to make a phone call. Instead I drive over to the tunnel and find no sign of him, nor do I find any leftover markings of a crime scene. The longer I sit with the possibility that he's hanging on for his life, the worse I feel about lying back and waiting for him to get help in his own time. Finally I get up the nerve to call the

City Desk to see what we know. I'm told that the guy they clubbed on Skid Row made it okay. He's been treated and released. But the guy beaten in the Third Street tunnel might not live. His name is Ernest Adams.

A weekend at a conference of the National Alliance on Mental Illness in Irvine does nothing to ease my fears about the risks facing Nathaniel, who was one tunnel and one block away from a beating. Dozens of attendees—many of them the relatives of people with mental illness—ask me how he's doing, and I tell them he's giving me a terrible scare. They understand. This group, which counts StigmaBuster Stella March as one of its pioneers, has become the largest advocacy and support group in the nation, and many of its members campaign to relax laws that make it difficult to forcibly treat someone who's mentally ill.

Carla Jacobs, an Orange County resident with short blond hair, a business suit and a look of fierce determination, sits me down in the lobby of the Irvine Marriott and tries to sign me up for the crusade. She tells me about her husband's delusional sister, who resisted treatment and was protected by existing laws, which prevented Jacobs and her husband from getting her the help they knew she needed. The tragedy that followed, she and her husband believe, was thoroughly preventable. The sister murdered her mother in a psychotic rage.

Jacobs pauses to let the weight of what she has just said sink in for me, then she puts it in context. California's 1968 Lanterman-Petris-Short Act ended involuntary commitments for people with mental disorders unless they were considered a danger to themselves or others, and it led to the emptying of the state's mental hospitals. In 2002, a year after a mentally ill man shot and killed three people in Nevada County, a new law gave counties the right to force "gravely disabled" mental patients into treatment if they were deemed unlikely to survive without supervision and couldn't provide their own food, clothing or shelter. But Laura's Law, named for one of the victims of the Nevada County shooting, was unfunded, challenged in court and seldom applied.

Get behind it, Jacobs implores, her gaze intense and unsettling. It's Nathaniel's only hope. What's more humane, after all? To respect someone's civil liberties to the point of allowing them to wither away on the street, or to intercede in the interest of their own welfare?

"He won't get better without treatment," she tells me, and he won't get treatment unless it's forced on him.

She may be right. But I walk away from our conversation, wondering how it would play out if Nathaniel were judged to be gravely disabled. Would a police car roll up, with officers chasing him and then carrying him away, kicking and screaming? Would a team of doctors come by with syringes and stab him with a sedative first? And would anything done forcibly make him more inclined, or less so, to trust authority and go along with a treatment plan over the long haul?

I take these questions across the hotel lobby to a nattily attired and neatly groomed Dr. Alex Kopelowicz, director of the San Fernando Valley Mental Health Clinic and a professor at UCLA. Kopelowicz, like Ragins, preaches recovery, but his model is more conventional. He strokes a close-cropped beard as he hears the latest with Nathaniel, and he's unsurprised by his roller-coaster ride or my exasperation. Kopelowicz says antipsychotic medication is one of several keys in a case like this, along with strong family support. His approach seems to be more about imposing a structured program on the patient, whereas Ragins tries to create a supportive environment in which the patient defines and manages his own recovery. The longer you go without treatment, Kopelowicz says, the harder it can be to go into remission and the less remission there will be.

So should I try to force him into treatment, as Carla Jacobs has just suggested?

Kopelowicz says he agrees with Jacobs that the pendulum has swung too far to the side of leaving people like Nathaniel to fend for themselves. He can't tell me what to do or what might work best for Nathaniel, but he says it is not unheard of for psychiatrists to advise loved ones to call the police and claim they've been threatened or assaulted. If a situation is dangerous and dire, and it's the only way to get treatment, it could save a life.

Is Nathaniel's situation dangerous or dire? Even without the Bumfights beating one block away, of course it is. I could even make the case that he is "gravely disabled," since he's unable to provide shelter for himself. But would either argument hold up in court? Probably not, given the high standard for proving incompetence and the reluctance of courts to infringe on civil rights.

For the rest of the two-day conference, I imagine myself dialing 911 to report that Nathaniel has threatened me. An actual injury might make it more believable, but what should I do, punch myself in the nose? Bang my head against the wall?

At the awards ceremony, I'm called to the stage and honored for the insights and public education I've provided with my columns about Nathaniel. I don't feel as though I've done much more than write about what people at the conference already know, and as I look out at a crowd that is standing and applauding, I'm tempted to grab the microphone and ask if anyone out there can tell me what to do next.

12

"You're going to have to leave the shopping cart at Lamp," I tell Nathaniel. "They're not going to let you roll that thing into Disney Hall."

"I've got that all taken care of," he insists. For days, he's been asking me if we're still going to see the Los Angeles Philharmonic, which he's now written on his T-shirt with a blue pen. He's worried that either I'm playing games with him or his mind is.

"I'll get you tomorrow morning at nine-thirty."

"Okay, Mr. Lopez."

"So what time am I picking you up?"

"Nine-thirty, right here in the courtyard."

"It's going to be a big day," I tell him.

"The anticipation is horrible," Nathaniel says.

. . .

The invitation began with Catherine Babcock, a Music Center publicist, who said we were welcome to attend a concert. Nathaniel was grateful for the offer but didn't want to be a distraction to paying customers. He said they shouldn't have to sit near a grubby, nappy-haired bum who goes weeks without bathing.

"You can shower at Lamp and I'll buy you some new things," I offered, but he still declined. I might have tried to talk him into it, but I had doubts about whether he could stay focused through an entire concert and whether he'd go into a panic about being trapped indoors with a couple thousand people. This was a man who preferred a patch of pavement to an apartment and dreaded the thought of being cooped up anywhere.

After telling Babcock thanks but no thanks, I called back with an idea.

What about a rehearsal?

Babcock referred me to Adam Crane, a publicist with the L.A. Philharmonic. Crane knew Nathaniel worshipped Beethoven and often visited the Pershing Square statue for inspiration, and it just so happened that Ludwig was the star of the 2005–2006 season. When I told Nathaniel that Crane had invited us to an early October rehearsal, he looked like he did on the day I brought him a new cello and violin. By the way, I said, they'll be working on Beethoven's Third Symphony.

"Symphony Number Three in E-Flat Major," he said, practically making the sign of the cross. "The *Eroica*."

"Have you played it yourself?" I asked.

"Yes. Many times."

"*I can't wear these* grubby things," Nathaniel says on the morning of the big day. He's got on burgundy sweatpants, a black T-shirt, a blue cardigan and white sneakers. "I've washed them over and over, and that's the best I seem to be able to do."

He stands in a corner of the Lamp courtyard next to his shopping cart, edgy, sweaty and crabby. This is a man who at his best has a way about him that could be called self-possessed or charismatic. There's a killer smile and a glint in his eye, sly and knowing. You can imagine him surrounded at a party, reciting Shakespeare and breaking down the interplay between violin and cello in *The Swan*. Then a switch goes off in his head and it's as if he's under a cloud, wondering if the rain is ever going to stop. Like he is now.

His right hand is wrapped with a dirty white rag. He tells me he got banged up in a fight, but he isn't in the mood to talk about it. The man I expected to find—spit-shined and ready to revisit Beethoven—is a no-show. I remind Nathaniel this is no ordinary day. We have a big event scheduled, and it's time to leave his shopping cart inside as we've agreed. But this is not the Nathaniel who found the anticipation unbearable.

"I can't leave it here," he snaps, making it sound personal, and I know we're in trouble now.

"Give me a minute and I'll see if I can talk to someone inside," I offer, but Nathaniel tells me not to bother wasting my time.

"I cannot leave my things with the rascals in there, who can*not* be trusted to do anything they're supposed to do."

This is our latest little dilemma. The place he comes to so he can get better is the source of new problems, and it's bringing out a dark side I seldom see when he's away from Skid Row and over by the tunnel. He's antisocial, doesn't like the way the agency is run and reserves his worst criticism for the people in charge.

"Mr. Stuart Robinson is not competent to manage Lamp, Los Angeles, Cleveland, New York City, LAPD, and I don't want any of those clowns in there telling me what to do when they cannot deal with the drug addicts and cigarette smokers who come in here and steal everything. They cannot be trusted, they will not be trusted, and I don't want anything to do with any of that nonsense. You can tell that to Los Angeles police chief William Bratton, Mayor Antonio Villaraigosa, the president of the United States of America, House of Representatives, U.S. Senate, Governor Arnold Schwarzenegger, the lieutenant governor of the state of California. A cockroach does not tell a greyhound what to do."

Maybe not, but more important, a columnist does not tell a paranoid schizophrenic what to do. Even if I could change his mind, what might we be in for at Disney Hall? I can't take him up there like this, and I'm angry with myself all over again for investing too much time in a losing proposition. I cut short my time with Caroline this morning once again—and left the house when Alison needed a break to concentrate on some work—so I could be with a man who is so sick he's sabotaging an adventure he eagerly anticipated for days.

"They're doing Beethoven's Third," I remind him, thinking

the mere mention of Beethoven's name will be like a spoonful of medicine.

"I am not going," he says. "If I have to miss all of that up there, I don't care. I don't need to go to Walt Disney Hall, Fantasia, Donald Duck, Beethoven. What I care about is this problem right here, that these people cannot be trusted to do their damn jobs. Does a cockroach talk to a greyhound? They cannot be trusted. Nobody here can be trusted and I am not leaving a thing in there with all the nonsense that goes on in this place. I wouldn't leave a *dog* here with those clowns."

Carla Jacobs is right. How will this ever change without medication? The chemical nature of his meltdown is so evident, even Tom Cruise could see it. Those neurotransmitters are sputtering, teasing out his anger, insecurity, paranoia. His muscles are flexed. His back is up. I'm going to give it one more try, using something I've never used on him before, and if that doesn't work I'll call it quits.

"We arranged this for your sake," I tell him. "It's Beethoven, and the orchestra has been kind enough to invite you up to Disney Hall so you can enjoy the thing you love most. It was very generous of them, and I think you should take advantage of this opportunity. If you don't want to do it for yourself, I'm asking you to do it for me. I'm your friend, and I've put a lot of time into this. I'd like you to do it."

No eye contact. He stares at the ground, and I can't begin to guess at the response I might get. The range of possibilities extends from him telling me to go to hell to him jumping into my car and humming Beethoven's Third all the way up the hill. Do I hold any sway over him? I'm too worn out to care. If he says to forget it, I'm prepared to walk away without another word, and I won't be back anytime soon.

Nathaniel finally brings his head up and there's a hint of contrition in his eye.

"Okay," he says. "I'll go. But I am not leaving my cart here."

I check my watch.

"Look," I tell him, "I've got my car here and I can't fit your shopping cart into it. I'm going to drive back to my office, and if you want to go to the rehearsal, I want you to push this cart over to my garage. I'll get someone to watch it for you, and then we're going to walk up to Disney Hall. But we're running out of time, and if you don't get moving right now we're not going to make it."

I'm firm to the point of being harsh, but I don't have a choice.

Nathaniel nods agreeably, but looks like a kid who has been ordered to eat his vegetables. I wait for him to get moving and then drive back to my office, hoping for the best. Fifteen minutes go by. No Nathaniel. Twenty minutes. Nothing. It's like having another child. I get back into the car to go looking for him but he's disappeared into the crowd. By day, Skid Row is swarming with shoppers looking for deals in the Toy District, at the flower markets and cheap variety stores. I try the Beethoven statue and the tunnel, then drive back to my office in defeat.

This must be what he put his family through. Jennifer is the only relative who checks in with me to see how he's doing, but, bound by obligations to work and family, she hasn't yet been able to visit her brother. I suppose she knows too much about how he broke their mother's heart over and over again with this very

behavior and worse, and she must feel a need to protect herself.
I feel jerked around, I feel sympathetic, I feel abused. It's almost
harder to see Nathaniel on the good days than the bad, because
you let yourself be deceived into thinking he's going to stay that
way. And then that switch goes off and he's fighting himself and
blaming it on everyone around him. I see now how someone really sick can burn through your patience, if not your sense of compassion. Not that I can forgive Nathaniel's father, who seems to
have written him off years ago. I don't know his situation in Las
Vegas, how he spends his days and nights, but if he's too busy to
pick up a phone and check on his son, why should I be out here
worrying about Nathaniel?

Whatever the answer, I do worry. And I can't just walk away.
Part of it is the desire to follow through on something that's become important and meaningful in my life, and to satisfy the
human instinct to help someone less fortunate. And maybe there's
something more.

The issue of race is inescapable for me. I often joke that the
main difference between the East Coast and the West is that
when I wrote columns for the *Philadelphia Inquirer*, the mail said Go
Back to Puerto Rico, and in Los Angeles it says Go Back to Mex-
ico. It's a strange phenomenon for someone with grandparents
from Italy and Spain, and it makes me more attuned to the hatred
aimed at people of color even in a place like Los Angeles, which
is defined by its multiculturalism. If I write about political observations at a black barbershop I frequent in South Central, there's
often e-mail from someone calling me a nigger-loving spic. E-
mail is a safe, convenient cover, the last refuge of the small-
minded and the profane. If I write about the Latino mayor in Los

Angeles, regardless of what I say, good or bad, I can expect mail calling me a kiss-ass Mexican sleazeball and apologist, or worse.

When I look at Nathaniel my thoughts flip back to a defining moment in high school, when I was hanging out with classmates in a park. One of the revelers had too much to drink and pounded his chest in a battle cry, announcing it was time to go kill some niggers. He had forgotten in his drunkenness that one of the kids among us was black. What has stuck with me through the years is not only the comment, but the look on the black kid's face.

I park the car in the Times garage and walk to the corner. Time to call Adam Crane and apologize, and then start the scavenger hunt for another column now that this one has bombed out. I look back over my shoulder one last time, but he's not there. The light changes and I look to the east.

There he is.

Nathaniel, with his knack for last-minute drama, has just turned the corner at Second and Main, with the two palm fronds sticking up out of the grill. If he puts up a fight about leaving his cart with the parking lot attendant, that'll be the end of it. But Nathaniel surprises me. He thanks the guard, grabs a violin out of the buggy and off we go.

I don't know what happened between Lamp and here, but he's relaxed now, the circular diatribes put away for the moment. We pass the corner where we've spent so much time just hanging out and talking, and he looks around to reset his bearings. The tunnel, the L.A. Times building and, up ahead, Disney Hall.

"You know," I tell him, "I've got tickets to see the National Symphony later this month. I'll get to see Itzhak Perlman."

"Oh my God," he says. "He's like molten lava on violin."

A half hour earlier I was with a madman. Now I'm with my own personal professor of music appreciation. Disney Hall floats above us, its metallic wings radiating late-morning light. "An iron butterfly," Nathaniel says. From paranoia to poetry, sirens to violins, madness to genius. Nathaniel's life is opera.

Disney Hall is the crown jewel in downtown L.A.'s attempt to reinvent itself after years of shabby desolation. The music center project had been foundering despite a $50 million donation from the wife of Walt Disney, but local philanthropist Eli Broad stepped in after her death and willed the Gehry-designed hall into existence, with a grand opening in 2003. Unfortunately this civic energy and vision of new beginnings did not extend just down the hill to Skid Row, and downtown L.A. was now a lady with a glittering crown and shabby boots. Nathaniel, up from the flats, hits the top of the hill at Grand Avenue and First Street and walks up to the performance schedule, running his hand over the board and pausing at the names of the composers who visit his dreams. "There's Beethoven," he says.

I'm still worried about how it might go inside. Adam Crane sounds like a perfectly nice gent on the phone, but how will he react if the Nathaniel of an hour ago reappears? I worry that Nathaniel will feel out of place or claustrophobic, but we're here now, heading up the stairs to the artists' entrance.

Crane marches confidently toward us, no sign of any qualms about meeting a man with mental illness. He greets Nathaniel as if he were a dignitary. I know the publicist played cello for years but chose not to go the conservatory route, and I get the sense he's impressed by Nathaniel not just for his story of survival, but because of his success as a musician, as far as it went.

"Would you like a tour?" Crane asks, handing Nathaniel a sou-venir copy of Frank Gehry's book on Disney Hall. He offers to carry it for him, but Nathaniel has already tucked it under his arm and doesn't want to let go of it.

Crane reminds Nathaniel that the orchestra will be rehearsing Beethoven's Third.

"The *Eroica*," Nathaniel says. "Are they rehearsing each movement?"

Indeed they are, Crane assures him. But there's just enough time for a VIP tour before we enter the hall.

"When's the last time you were in a concert hall?" I ask Na-thaniel.

"I haven't been in a concert hall in four billion years," he says. He's relaxed and in good spirits. The smile is back, broad and gracious, and he speaks with a self-assured tone of formality. A continental in sweatpants.

Crane marches us into elevators and stairwells, passionately delivering the history of the construction and the little quirks of the place. The floral design on the carpet, for instance, was a trib-ute to Mrs. Lillian Disney and her love of flowers. On the sixth floor, we exit a semi-secret doorway to an outdoor landing.

"This is one of my favorite places in Disney Hall," Crane says, leading us along a narrow path with the muted stainless steel panels of the roof rising above us. It's like sneaking around in the folds of a lily.

Crane checks his watch and herds us back into an elevator.

"We're right behind the stage right now," he says as we enter a room with a sloped ceiling, the terraced rows of seats above us in the hall.

"It's like a dream," Nathaniel says. "I don't know if this is a dream or purgatory."

And I don't know how he means that. Maybe just as it sounds. It's a place just short of where he so badly wanted to be.

We enter a long hallway near the musicians' locker rooms and a voice comes over the PA system, startling Nathaniel.

"That sounds like the voice from Cleveland psychiatric," he says and in a way, yes, it does seem that Disney Hall may be his new hospital.

He asks Crane if he knows Yo-Yo Ma, and if so, is he a likable guy?

Quite, says Crane, but before he can say much more Nathaniel has switched subjects. He and Crane are sharing thoughts on conductors James Conlon, Lorin Maazel and Herbert von Karajan. I don't have anything to add to that conversation, so I ask Nathaniel if he's aware that Mr. Crane is a cellist.

"Do you know Dvořák's Cello Concerto?" Nathaniel asks.

"It's one of my favorites," says Crane, telling Nathaniel he owns a Czechoslovakian cello made in 1875.

"I don't want to mess with it," Nathaniel says jocularly. "I don't even want to look at it."

I don't know if he's slyly fishing for an invitation to give it a try, but if so, it works.

Crane takes us to his office and brings out the cello.

"May I?" Nathaniel asks.

"Please. Go ahead."

It takes him a few minutes to tune up, and then he begins playing pizzicato, plucking strings with his bandaged right hand.

Crane and I share a glance and a smile. Nathaniel is playing Bach's Cello Suite No. 1: Prelude, and eventually picks up the bow to give that a go. As he plays, orchestra staffers wander out of their offices to the sound of the Pied Piper. They stand outside the glass-walled office, looking in at the strange sight of a homeless man making beautiful music. Nathaniel seems oblivious, though I wouldn't be surprised if I was wrong.

"He's got it," Crane whispers.

It's reassuring to get this assessment from a musician. Although I hear some of his more obvious mistakes, I also know Nathaniel's sound is the baring of his soul, and that when he closes his eyes, as he's doing now, it's as if he's come to a clearing in a forest and found relief under an open sky.

Nathaniel deflects the compliments from staffers as we make our way toward the hall, stopping at an entryway marked "Stage Level Door 1."

"Are you ready?" asks Crane.

We push through and into the warm yellow light of the wood-paneled hall Gehry has described as a living room for the city of Los Angeles. The massive pipe organ looks like a Disney-inspired explosion of sound, with six thousand flutes of Norwegian pine and Douglas fir teetering over the stage. The bowl itself is more intimate than the flamboyant exterior would suggest, and it feels like we're in the belly of a violin or cello, with two thousand seats clinging to the sides of the sound box. Nathaniel gives the hall a cursory look, but his gaze is fixed on the stage, with the musicians filing back in from the dressing room. One of them sees us and comes bounding toward Nathaniel.

"I'm Pete Snyder," says the cellist, a thirty-three-year member of the orchestra. Snyder shakes Nathaniel's hand and says he's read all about him.

"János Starker," Nathaniel says, noting a resemblance to the bald, Hungarian-born cellist. Nathaniel says he's more than a little impressed by the mustachioed Snyder's thirty-three-year stint with a great orchestra. Hands clasped in front of him, suavely collegial, Nathaniel tells Snyder that his mentor, Mr. Harry Barnoff, put in forty-six years with the Cleveland Orchestra.

"I want to compliment you as well," Snyder says, telling Nathaniel he has his own accomplishment of note—namely his survival on the streets just down the hill.

"I just want to play," Nathaniel says. "I'll live underneath a rock."

We take a seat in the center of the hall, alone but for a few staffers. It's like having a private concert.

"They look so happy," Nathaniel says as the musicians tune their instruments and the conductor, Esa-Pekka Salonen, strides onto the stage under a bob of blond hair. "I would be happy, too, if I was going to play the Third Symphony, especially with good players. You look over at the next player and say, 'Wow.'"

Napoleon Bonaparte was the original inspiration for Beethoven's Third Symphony, but as legend has it, the composer's opinion of the man changed when he saw the liberator become a tyrant. He called his symphony *Eroica*, which means heroic, and intended it as a tribute to courage rather than to a single man. This is information I've gotten from Nathaniel, a patient teacher who seems to enjoy being able to offer me the gift of his knowledge. The *Eroica* begins with two short blasts that blow you back into your seat. Then, having gotten your attention, Beethoven gets the string sections going with a conversation that swoons and swells. There's romance and suspense in the piece, the anticipation of a bold and defining statement. But for me, the best part of the show is Nathaniel, who is on the edge of his seat, following along on the sheet music in his head. Slack-jawed, mesmerized, emancipated, he pulls out an imaginary baton, giggles and sways. The Third was once described as a composition in which dark clouds dissolve into sunshine. I wonder if this is what makes Beethoven Nathaniel's god of creation. The second movement tiptoes into the hall like a rumor of death, and Nathaniel brings a shoulder into me and cups his hand to my ear.

"He's in the room," he says. "If his spirit was in the room, it would be somewhere around there. Do you see the conductor? That's Beethoven. He will interpret Beethoven. He *is* Beethoven."

I don't know if he means it literally or figuratively, but any distinction fades into meaninglessness. Beethoven's music is a portrait of Nathaniel's imagination. There's high drama and contradiction, a collision of opposing forces, lyrical respites. Each note is as true today as it will always be, and for Nathaniel the music is both medicine and muse, no less an inspiration now than it was before his fall.

"They are flawless, flawless, flawless players," he whispers. "Every single note is there. There's not any nonsense. Of course, this is a world-renowned orchestra."

For which, at the end of Beethoven's emotional endurance test, he has one word.

"Bravo!"

Crane hurries us backstage to meet Esa-Pekka Salonen. The

conductor accepts Nathaniel's compliments with bashful grace, and Nathaniel walks away still trying to pronounce his name. He meets next with Ben Hong, a close friend of Crane's and assistant principal cellist. Hong, born in Taiwan, was a Juilliard student, too, and Nathaniel feels compelled to admit he didn't make it all the way through. What is it like, Nathaniel wants to know, to hear an audience respond appreciatively to the music you create? Feels good, Hong tells him, and next Nathaniel wants to know about the challenges of Beethoven's Third. "It's emotionally and physically exhausting," Hong says, and the two of them kibitz about conductors, composers and the genius of Beethoven.

I step back when the conversation goes over my head and enjoy the sight of Nathaniel handling himself so smoothly. He seems back in his element and almost a student again, chatting up a classmate in the hall during a break. He lives in two distant constellations, this man who fends off rats on Skid Row and holds forth at Disney Hall, mingling easily with members of the orchestra. I suffer no illusions, because I know he's a very sick man, even though Adam Crane, Pete Snyder and Ben Hong probably don't realize the full extent of it. Maybe he'll be motivated to keep their acquaintance, and if so, I can use it to advance his recovery as much as that's possible. If he moves indoors, cleans up and gets stabilized, it will make more visits to Disney Hall possible and put him closer to the music he lives for. He considers me his friend, after all. How can I not keep trying, given the distance we've traveled in a single day?

We say good-bye to Ben Hong and head down toward the stage on the way to the exits. I notice again that Nathaniel has been carrying his violin all this time and I assume it was to prove his membership in the brotherhood. But I see something else in his eyes as he climbs into the seats behind the stage, just beneath the pipe organ, and opens his violin case. Nathaniel lifts the instrument to the crease between shoulder and chin. Disney Hall is empty when he begins playing, although in Nathaniel's mind, Beethoven might still be lingering in the shadows.

Part Two

13

Just up the street from Nathaniel's courtyard hangout at Lamp, I watch two prostitutes work the corner of Sixth and San Julian on a warm October evening. It seems fairly obvious that the short heavy one is the madam and the tall skinny one with a severe limp is one of her girls. The former calls herself T.J., for Thick and Juicy, and the other is T.T., for Tall and Tiny. Business is booming, as one john after another approaches. There's nothing remarkable about prostitution in a big city, but this operation has two features that make it noteworthy. First, there's a police station one block away. Second, the prostitutes do their business in outhouses.

For me, there's no more telling illustration of Skid Row as a rock-bottom depository. It's been written off, shoved beyond public consciousness and left to wallow in its own lawlessness and despair. A Vietnam or World War II amputee can fall out of his wheelchair in the middle of the street, a filthy colostomy bag next to him, and people will walk by as if he isn't there. An insane man walks naked through the rubble and few people take notice. Heroin addicts pump needles into their arms without a glance toward the Central District police headquarters. A barefoot woman with her top falling off runs down San Julian screaming hysterically, batting away ghosts.

This is where Nathaniel sleeps. He may be paranoid, but when he rails against lawlessness and disorder, and when he tells me drug dealers and thieves are out to take everything he's got, is he being crazy or observant?

Skid Row is an old story. It's so old no one has cared to revisit it for years, but my *Times* colleagues Cara Mia DiMassa and Richard Winton are beginning to hit it hard. There's a new twist this time—the collision of opposing forces. One feature of the downtown renaissance is the conversion of dilapidated buildings into swanky lofts, boutique shops and upscale restaurants. Development and decay are becoming neighbors on Skid Row, and money is competing with misery.

There's a lot I can't do for Nathaniel. I can't cure him. I can't make him see a doctor. I can't take him home to Cleveland or get him into an orchestra. But now that he's a character in the life of the city, a man people have come to care about, maybe there's a service in reminding people what we do with those among us who are too sick to care for themselves. Don't sweeten it, my editor, Sue Horton, tells me. Serve it up for breakfast raw and unfiltered. Tell people what Nathaniel is up against, and shake a fist at City Hall.

· · ·

It's 11:18 in the morning when the call comes in. Possible over-dose. Firefighter-paramedic Dave Chavez, forty-two, grabs a blank incident report and marches toward his Rescue 9 ambulance with partner Juan Penuelas. At 11:20, they pull out of the station. From the back of the ambulance, Chavez is taking in the devastation through the windows. People stumble and rant, they lie in filth. Nothing surprises Chavez, who has spent ten years at what has long been one of the busiest stations in the United States. Fires are an old-fashioned rarity for Chavez and his colleagues. But thirty, forty, fifty times a shift, they get called out on cases just like this one. We travel only half a block, to where a woman is sprawled on the pavement. Her friends close in when Chavez steps out of the ambulance, and some of them don't look much better than she. They're skeletal, faces full of shadows, skin pocked and ulcer-ated by needles. They tell Chavez the woman is about twenty-five and shot up about ten hours ago right here in this very spot. The street has its own social order. Crack addicts line the west side and heroin addicts the east. In the middle of the block is Lamp.

Once again I wonder if I'm the one, not Nathaniel, who needs to have his head examined. I'm trying desperately to cajole him into leaving the area around the tunnel and spending his nights here at Lamp, which sits in the middle of one of the saddest blocks in the entire city of four million people. LAPD chief William Bratton has called this area "the worst situation in America." And yet it's the only place near downtown where Na-thaniel can get the kind of help Lamp provides. I once suggested that Nathaniel let me take him to Long Beach, which has problems but not the teeming madness of Skid Row. There, I might be able to steer him in to see Dr. Ragins. Forget it, Nathaniel said. He's a creature of habit, and he feels more comfortable in the company of the devil he knows.

While Chavez checks the fallen woman, I quickstep across the street to see if Nathaniel is in. Although he's still sleeping at the tunnel, more and more of his days are spent in the courtyard.

"Oh, Mr. Lopez," he says.

"You doing okay?" I ask.

"Yes, sir. I'm fine."

"Just wanted to say hello, but I've got to go. I'm hanging out with these paramedics out here."

He comes to the doorway with his violin. It's gotten to where he won't let me leave without a half dozen attempts to keep the conversation going, raising his voice over mine as I say I've got to go. I point to the back of the ambulance, where Chavez and his partner are lifting the fallen woman up on a gurney. Nathaniel, who hears sirens day and night and has seen this very scene played out dozens of times, is disgusted.

"These drugs are killing everybody," he says.

Chavez is having trouble getting a blood pressure reading or an EKG. The woman is jerking around, squirming, wailing. Chavez sees that her tongue is dry and caked and that worries him. "I think she might have some other things on board besides heroin," he says. He wants to tap a vein and run an IV line in case she takes a turn for the worse on the short ride to County-USC Medical Center, but her arms and neck are covered with tracks. Her angular face, with strong cheekbones and spooky dark eyes, is a display of pain and panic, mostly the latter. She's too weak—or maybe too drugged out—to do anything but moan in a husky voice short of breath.

This is the drill for Chavez one shift after another, as he and his colleagues deal with the human wreckage caused by a thousand different failures. The housing market is obscene, health care is a luxury, addiction rehab is in short supply, the schools have shameful dropout rates, the service economy doesn't pay a living wage, the notorious L.A. gangs are selling drugs outside twelve-step programs, the psychiatric emergency room is jammed and mental health services like the ones at Lamp are few and far between. Chavez gets through the day by not giving a thought to any of the things that are out of his control, by passing judgment on no one and by not letting any of the clients get to him, whether he saves their lives or watches them die.

"I try to treat everyone the way I'd want to be treated," he tells me. "You meet some of the nicest, most interesting people out here."

The woman without a name begins to fade as we approach the hospital. She looks up with eyes wide and filled with fear, but they quickly go milky and then blank.

"She's circling," Chavez yells to his driver, which means to hit the gas because she's going down the drain.

The two of them muscle her out of the ambulance and push the gurney toward the building, exploding through the doors and into the emergency room, where a team of ten doctors and attendants work on her.

"Clear," says a doctor, delivering a jolt that lifts her off the gurney.

She's on her back, eyes still open but empty. A few feet away, another OD victim is unconscious, and next to him is a man who has taken a fall and is being examined for a possible broken back and neck.

"Three hundred. Clear. Three-sixty. Clear."

Chavez watches from ten feet away, pulling for her. They get a rhythm briefly, then lose it.

"She's gone," Chavez says, and moments later they wrap her in a white plastic sheet with her eyes still open, clearing the way for another overdose case and a teenage stabbing victim, covered in blood, who will be dead in minutes.

When we get back to the station, I walk over and tell the twenty-five-year-old woman's friends the news, figuring no one else will. They gasp and shudder, but it's not clear if that's because she meant something to them or because they know they're on the same journey. I walk across the street to look for Nathaniel, but he's long gone, out there somewhere with his shopping cart and his instruments in a downtown of dark, bottomless depths.

A couple of nights later and just up the street, a half block from where the twenty-five-year-old woman was loaded into the ambulance for her last ride, T.J. is weeping. When you're a prostitute in an outhouse, there are no good days. But this one has been worse than most. She says a man died in the outhouse a few hours earlier and was taken away by paramedics. It was a friend and she doesn't know what happened. When the door of the outhouse opens just enough, I can see clothes on hangers draped along the sides, and a radio, and some toiletries. T.J. doesn't just work in the outhouse. She lives in it.

It's an open secret on Skid Row that some Porta Potties are not being put to their intended purpose. Drugs, sex, housing. Anything goes. T.J. insists her outhouse is only an occasional residence, reserved for when she works too late to get home to Inglewood. She shows me where she stores her shoes and fishnet stockings and fancy hats, and she demonstrates how she covers the toilet bench at night and curls up on top of it to sleep. This is the outhouse where her friend died earlier in the day, on the street that has claimed two victims in the last forty-eight hours.

While I'm talking to her a rat comes up from the sewers. It runs past a discarded brassiere, a tossed apple core and an empty Fritos bag. The rats are a common sight in and around the Porta Potties, which do on occasion get put to their intended use, as an overpowering stench suggests. But there are those who refuse to enter the stalls and instead squeeze between and behind them to do their business. This explains the hot rivers of urine on the pavement.

The mayor of Los Angeles is on the phone. He's been reading my page-one series on Skid Row, finds the details unsurprising but shocking nonetheless, and wants to know if he can come join me as I make my rounds. My first instinct is to politely decline. Mayor Antonio Villaraigosa has rock-star status. He turns heads and he travels with a police detail. I don't need any of that while trying to discreetly approach subjects on Skid Row and get them

to open up to me. Then again, this is precisely the kind of attention I'd hoped Nathaniel's story would attract. There's probably
no one who could make more of a difference here than the mayor.
Villaraigosa tells me he's on the road, but he's going to go home
and get rid of his suit, so he'll blend in a little better.

Villaraigosa has a weakness that could work to the benefit of
Nathaniel and hundreds like him. The mayor can't help but want
to save the world. He wants to take over the school district, end
poverty, build affordable housing, hire thousands more police officers, bust up gangs. Despite his inhuman energy, he can't do all
of that any more than he can annex Santa Barbara, but I can't
imagine the mayor seeing what's out here in all its disturbing
detail and turning a cold shoulder. I suspect he takes personally
the fact that so lawless and sorrowful a place as Skid Row exists
just a few blocks from his City Hall office. Like mayors before
him, he's aware of the problems, but there's been little political
advantage in doing something about them because they haven't
been spread across page one of the newspaper in quite this way,
an indictment of indifference and a call to conscience. New York
City answered the call several years earlier, investing in housing
and services that cleared the streets. San Francisco is well ahead
of Los Angeles, too, and Villaraigosa doesn't suffer negative com-
parisons well.

A *slow, steady drizzle* is falling when the mayor arrives in jeans
and hooded jacket. Few people recognize him under the hood, so
he's able to get a close and anonymous look at the two hundred

people huddled outside the Midnight Mission. This is the over-flow crowd, the ones who won't get a cot inside. The luckier ones have wedged in under the overhang, where they can at least keep their blankets and bagged belongings dry. The mayor talks to a woman in her sixties who says she was put out of a hotel when a housing voucher ran out. She's in a wheelchair pushed by her husband, a Vietnam vet, and says they've got to wait a month for another ticket to sleep indoors. After hearing their story the mayor goes inside, where he meets with a young woman and her two children, all of them getting settled on cots in a room with a hundred others. She's got an abusive husband and nowhere else to go, she says as the kids curl up and try to sleep in this room full of strangers.

Later in the evening I'm at the corner of Seventh and San Julian, across the street from Dave Chavez's fire station. I'm talking to several men in wheelchairs when I feel a presence over my shoulder. Chavez told me there was once a knife fight, at this very location, in which one of the combatants was stabbed, walked slowly across the street for help and collapsed at the door of the fire station. I'm on one knee with my notepad out, an easy target for someone who's deranged or high or angry that a stranger is here asking personal questions. I turn just enough to see if I'm safe, and realize it's the mayor. While he stands watching, one of the men, squatting on the pavement next to a man in a wheelchair, takes a syringe and jabs it into the crease of his own left arm. His body goes slack and his eyes roll as the heroin races through his veins. The mayor watches in stony silence on a rainy night.

Within days the outhouses at Sixth and San Julian are gone,

carted away by city workers. By week's end, the mayor adds Skid Row to his fix-it list.

"I am going to take on the challenge," he says. "I mean, that almost looked like Bombay or something, except with more violence. There is no place [in the city] where the chaos and degradation are as pronounced. You see a complete breakdown of society."

The mayor pledges to shift an additional $50 million into housing and other services on Skid Row and beyond. Two City Council members pile on, announcing their own plan to end homelessness. For the first time in years, the calamity on Skid Row is front and center, due in no small part to Nathaniel, whose story made it impossible to ignore. But pledges are cheap, and New York City's annual budget for housing and services is three times that of Los Angeles, even if the mayor comes through on his $50 million promise. What will any of this mean for Nathaniel?

14

———◆———

Casey Horan, the director of Lamp, isn't always easy to read. But Shannon Murray can't hide what she's thinking. She's quietly seething, ticked off at something I've just said. The three of us are on a bus with Darrell Steinberg and other members of the state commission whose job it is to figure out how to best spend more than $1 billion a year in California on expanded mental health services. The bus is pulling away from Lamp on a tour of various programs, and Steinberg is talking about the success of places like Lamp and the Village, suggesting that more funding will translate to more people being lured off the streets and into housing with supportive services that help them rebuild their lives.

Don't be so sure of it, I'm telling him. Nathaniel continues to resist help despite months of effort by me and Lamp employees. He's as delusional as he was on the day I met him, and his latest hallucination is that an *L.A. Times* guard poured water into one of his violins and ruined it while we were at Disney Hall. Nathaniel insists it's proof that no one on this earth can be trusted and he'll never be able to return to Disney Hall. I'm coming around to the conclusion that if Nathaniel's ever going to have a chance of getting better, he's going to have to be forcibly treated.

Murray, with straight reddish hair and a look of weary disdain, glares at me. Together, she and Horan have decades of experience. They've improved the lives of hundreds of people with mental illness and I've just stumbled into the game, parading my talented musician across the pages of the *Los Angeles Times* and trying to pass myself off as an authority to Darrell Steinberg, the godfather of the landmark proposition that created the windfall for mental health funding. Murray elbows her way into the conversation to say that I've got it all wrong.

"We're so close," she says, noting that on the day she and Patricia Lopez answered my call and met Nathaniel near the tunnel, he wanted no part of Lamp. Now, she says, he's there practically every day and is often the first one at the door in the morning. "That's a huge step for someone who's been out on his own for so many years," she argues. "You just have to be more patient."

Rushing things, Horan chimes in, would be disastrous. Tall and thin, with short, sandy-colored hair, she's more diplomatic than Murray but no less intense. When she speaks, she appears to be summoning all her strength to keep from lashing out.

"You've built up all this trust with him," she says, telling me that if I were to now force him to do something against his will, I could drive him away for good, and he's likely to get worse. "Being restrained and having a stranger take control over you is a terrifying, terrifying experience." For people who are violently ill, there's no alternative. "But this is Nathaniel," she says, reminding me of his humility and the gentle soul that hides behind a sometimes ornery twin. "He's coming around in his own way, and it has to be that way. With us supporting him and earning his trust. Otherwise you could lose him forever."

Patience, they say. October is gone and we're halfway through November. Before much longer a year will have gone by, and the questions and answers are still the same. Has he moved inside? Is he on his meds?

Horan and Murray are still convinced Nathaniel is close to trading his tunnel for an apartment, so much so that they're holding on to one that has just become available in a residential complex that abuts the back side of the Lamp property. If he takes the room, he'll be able to wake up in the morning and walk through a back breezeway to breakfast. Then he can play music in the courtyard, and maybe—it could take a while, of course—he'll decide one day that he'd like to start meeting with Dr. Prchal.

It all makes for a lovely picture, except that Nathaniel is as militantly opposed as ever. "I have no interest in putting my possessions in a room where the biggest thieves in the world can come and steal everything I own. It is not going to happen. Not now and not ever, and I don't care if I have to appeal my case to the president of the United States or Stevie Wonder, but I'll do whatever it takes to keep people from messing with me and my things," he insists.

My counterarguments accomplish nothing other than to add

a few more gray hairs to my balding head. Why does he have to be bothered with any of this, Nathaniel asks, when he keeps insisting he prefers to live outside and sleep in the tunnel? Beethoven is out there, isn't he? "I'm not leaving him out there alone."

The high of our trip to Disney Hall has begun to fade and Nathaniel is wearing me out. I'm still wired by training to work toward resolution, but every time I think I've tied a pretty bow on this story, it unravels. Though I care more about Nathaniel now than ever, I'm beginning to resent the demands he puts on me, as well as the constant fear that he's going to get mugged for the instruments. He often needs a new string, or bridge repair, or sheet music, and of course I'm the one he calls. I juggle my schedule to pick up a broken instrument, juggle again to retrieve it from the repair shop and lose a good chunk of another day tracking him down and returning the goods. I'm stealing time from writing columns and I'm stealing time from my family, and although Alison is being more patient than I would be in her shoes, I'm beginning to feel as though something's got to give. And I know it can't be my job or my time with family.

As the winter of my discontent settles in, Nathaniel goes about his days and nights with little awareness of my angst, and there's no visible sign that colder weather is going to change his mind about shelter. I drive through the tunnel in the morning and see him playing at Second and Hill as if he hasn't a care in the world. If he hasn't eaten breakfast at Lamp, he'll go to a free breakfast line in the Toy District or use one of the donations from his fans to buy a packet of sandwich cookies and a cup of coffee. For him, the toughest decision in a day is figuring out whether to play his original violin, the new one or the cello. To shake things up, he'll push his cart over to the Central Library, pay someone to guard it and lug all three of his instruments inside to copy sheet music.

At Second and Hill, he's gotten creative with the drab, nondescript slab where he kills so many hours each day. He uses tape and string to post Asian-language newspapers or travel magazine photos to the trunks of palm trees. I half expect to see him out there one day in a Hawaiian shirt, swinging on a hammock while he fans himself with palm fronds or strums a ukulele. In the evening, I drive by and see him at the other end of the tunnel, taping U.S. flags to signposts or impersonating a conductor. He routinely carries on animated conversations without a partner present, which I suppose has its advantages. I drive home, wrung out after another deadline-crashing day, mouth dry, traffic miserable. And he's in the tunnel, blissfully fiddling his way through the Elgar Cello Concerto.

Not that I would ever diminish or romanticize a dreadful illness, but anticipating the possibility that this will forever be his life, and looking for an excuse to leave him to his ways, I find myself asking what might sound like a strange question.

Is he happy?

Clearly music makes him happy, and how many musicians in the world have as much time to play as he does, entirely free of expectation? For him, it isn't work. Sure, he gets down on himself occasionally, frustrated by his limitations. But he doesn't have to worry about training for an audition, like he did when he was younger, and he doesn't need to earn a living at it. For Nathaniel, music is freedom. Now that the Little Pedro's Blue Bongo gig is a thing of the past, if he makes mistakes or finds himself stuck in a rut, he has to answer only to himself and the Beethoven statue.

Nathaniel will probably never be happy on my terms or by my definition, but maybe that's my problem rather than his. Does he have a big fat mortgage hanging over his head, with twenty-seven years to go on the first and twenty-five on the home equity line of credit, which is set at prime plus one and constantly spiking? I make good money for a newspaper guy and we live very nicely, but the crazy California real estate market eats a big chunk of my take-home, and Alison has cut back on her work to enjoy Caroline's early years. At the rate the newspaper staff is shrinking, we're fast approaching a time when I'm the only one left to serve as editor, and my first order from Chicago would probably be to lay myself off.

Nathaniel doesn't have to worry about a daughter who will be just fifteen when he hits retirement age. His computer doesn't crash. He doesn't have to call his HMO six hundred times to scream about a doctor bill it refuses to cover. He doesn't have to call a bank and threaten to strangle someone over a "thorough investigation" that has determined I was lying when I reported a case of identity theft and the loss of $3,000. Nathaniel is 100 percent off the books. No Social Security card, no driver's license, no address, no living will, no job, no lawn to mow, no phone call to return, no retirement to plan for and no rules except his own.

The day of the Beethoven rehearsal, we walked one block down from Disney Hall and he told me he had to go to the bathroom.

"Just hold on," I said. "My office is only a block away and you can go there."

"Mr. Lopez," he said, looking at me like a six-year-old, "I can't wait."

"Well, why didn't you go back at Disney Hall?" I asked.

"I didn't think of it," he said. "But I really have to go bad."

Across the street was the Los Angeles County Courthouse. In the garden was a tree. Nathaniel made a dash for it, returning a minute later with a look of great relief.

How can I ever reel him back to the world of rules and regulations, of protocol and privies? He is tied to nothing but his passion and the world it delivers him into, a world in which the city is his orchestra and the conductor is a statue. He sees a swaying palm and hears violins. A bus roars by and gives him a bass line. He hears footsteps and imagines Beethoven and Brahms out for a stroll.

"I can't survive," he once told me of his refusal to come indoors, "if I can't hear the orchestra the way I like to hear it."

15

Patience is no doubt a wonderful virtue, but mendacity has its advantages as well. If Nathaniel wouldn't move into the apartment Lamp reserved for him, maybe he would at least consider using it as a music studio. And to seduce him into giving it a try, I now have the perfect bait. Peter Snyder, the Los Angeles Philharmonic cellist who shook Nathaniel's hand at Disney Hall, has e-mailed me with an offer.

"After I met Nathaniel, it left me with such a hole or void in the center of my chest that I started to think about how lucky I've been with my life in general. It so moved me that I simply have to do something to change what the future Nathaniels out there have to face. . . . Perhaps if he knew that I wanted to help him, he might be more inclined to seek a more permanent solution. What do you think?"

When I call, Snyder says he's willing to give Nathaniel free lessons, orchestra schedule permitting. This is where I get the bold idea to bring him in on a white lie. I tell Snyder about the apartment Nathaniel refuses to move into and ask if he's willing to give him lessons there. We can tell Nathaniel lessons aren't allowed at Disney Hall, there's nowhere to do it at the *L.A. Times* and there's no quiet space at Lamp. Snyder likes the idea and agrees to play along.

"Nathaniel, I've got some terrific news," I tell him at Second and Hill. "Do you remember Mr. Snyder from the orchestra?"

"Peter Snyder," he says. "Yeah, he looked like János Starker."

"Well, guess what. János Starker wants to give you lessons."

His eyes brighten.

"At Disney Hall?" he asks.

"He says he can't do it there. He wants to do it in your apartment."

Nathaniel squirms.

"Why can't we do it at Disney Hall? It's the Beethoven hall, the home of Beethoven, the Los Angeles Philharmonic."

"They've got lots of activities up there and they don't have a room where he could meet with you regularly."

"Then we could do it here," Nathaniel says.

Here? We can barely hear each other speak over the traffic, and the tunnel acts like a megaphone.

"I just don't think Mr. Snyder would go for it," I say, raising my voice a bit louder than necessary to accentuate the noise factor Mr. Snyder would be up against. "I'd suggest my office, but there's not a place there where you could have any privacy. And the Lamp courtyard wouldn't work, with people coming and going all the time."

He agrees those options are no good, but I don't quite have him snookered yet.

"Your apartment is the only place we could think of. Mr. Snyder said he'll need a quiet place or it's just not going to be worth his time or yours."

"It's not my apartment," he insists, copping an attitude. "I don't have an apartment and I don't need an apartment. I don't want to have anything to do with it. It is not my apartment."

It feels as if we've been here too many times before. Should I beg? Should I throw my hands up and walk away? Such a waste. Is he too sick to have any idea how rare an opportunity this is?

"I don't want to see you blow this chance," I tell him. "How many years have you been playing music without the benefit of someone who could help you get better? Hasn't it been thirty years? Now you've got a cellist from one of the great orchestras of the world volunteering to give you lessons. For free! This is a lucky break, Nathaniel. I don't want to waste Mr. Snyder's time and I know you don't, either. So why don't we just try it in the apartment one time, and if you don't want to continue with it, we'll call the whole thing off?"

It's the latest do-or-die moment for us. I'm sorry, but Mollie Lowery and Mary Scullion were nuns, and I don't have their fortitude. Nathaniel, fortunately, is a very bright man. I'd say he's probably in on the lie. But he picks up on something in my voice or sees something in my body language that tells him what's at stake here.

"All right," he finally says.

I don't know what he wants more—the lesson, or to hold on to our friendship.

. . .

It seems I should try to make Nathaniel comfortable with the apartment before I bring Snyder around, so I call Stuart Robinson at Lamp and he arranges to let me in. By now, I feel awkward about calling Robinson or anyone else at Lamp. They have dozens of Nathaniels, and while they appreciate my relationship with him, I know I'm putting them in a bind. Would they hold an apartment open for several weeks for someone who isn't written about regularly in the paper? Probably not, and they have to wrestle with the morality of keeping a bed reserved for him while turning away people who need help just as much as he does. They also have to deal with the public exposure of their private work with a man who is mentally ill. At times, Nathaniel is one of their more difficult clients. He endlessly chastises fellow clients, lets loose bigoted tirades and maligns Robinson for offering safe harbor to those who cuss, smoke or otherwise violate his sense of civility. In other words, Nathaniel is a burden, bringing with him the added pressure for Lamp employees of proving their effectiveness. And yet the mild-mannered Robinson politely returns my calls and is slowly building his own relationship with Nathaniel, and he goes along with the idea of using lessons from Pete Snyder as an enticement to get Nathaniel into the apartment.

Nathaniel is in a front corner of the courtyard when I drop by, talking to himself next to his packed and ready-to-go cart. Okay, so we're off to a decent start. Nathaniel is tapping on his tarp-covered heap with a pair of sticks, and he tells me this is his first love. He's a drummer, not a man of strings. Therefore, he doesn't need Snyder and we can forget the lessons in the apartment.

Good Lord. I don't have time for this.

Mr. Snyder's not here today, I tell him firmly. It's just the two of us, and we're going to the apartment.

"I'm sure he's a fabulous player, Mr. Snyder, like Harry Barnoff, Jim Brown, Mickey Mantle, all fabulous players. Colonel Sanders, Johnny Carson. Why not statues of those characters? Why do they have the military statues in Cleveland and not in Los Angeles, where someone had the inspiration to put the Beethoven statue in Pershing Square? I'm sure Mr. Snyder is excellent. I know he's an excellent player, a magnificently accomplished professional musician, because I saw him playing Beethoven's Third Symphony. He's a professional, all right. He's almost Yo-Yo Ma. Do you think Yo-Yo Ma is a nice man? Because Adam Crane said he's a really good guy, but I don't know. I haven't seen the youngster since Juilliard, and he wouldn't remember me."

Each time I interrupt, he cuts me off. I finally get his attention long enough to say it's time to go check out the apartment. Robinson will take the shortcut through the back, but Nathaniel's cart won't fit through the hall at Lamp, so we're going to walk around the corner and meet Robinson on the other side.

There's still a cluster of flowers in the spot where the twenty-five-year-old woman spent the last hours of her life, and there's no sign that the crack trade has slowed on the opposite side of the street. A man with only one shoe is lighting a crack pipe, and a dealer shoots us a what-are-you-looking-at glance. Nathaniel returns a cold stare. At Sixth Street, the corner is naked without the Porta Potties, but a dozen people are still milling about or lying flat on the ground. With his hubcap as a shield and violin bow as a sword, Nathaniel is a bit like Don Quixote, holding to a strict moral and artistic code while everyone around him has fallen. I feel like Sancho Panza, defending the honor of a man who knows so little of his own frailty. As we cut left on the almost satirically named Wall Street, Nathaniel holds up the procession to grab a dustpan and broom from his cart so he can clear the cigarette butts, syringes and empty cans. He tosses the mess into one of his five-gallon saddlebags and we continue along a street that's a far nicer sight than San Julian. Trees make the difference. Trees, and the fact that no one has fallen face-first into rotting trash.

"This looks really nice," I say in a most encouraging tone. "Clean, quiet."

Nathaniel picks up another soda can and a potato-chip wrapper, which I find encouraging. He's already taking over the sanitation contract on this street.

The Ballington, a plum-colored two-story apartment building, has a wheelchair entrance that's perfect for a shopping cart. Everything is falling into place, or so I'd like to think. Nathaniel pushes up the ramp and at the top, the automatic doors slide open, as if his arrival has been anticipated.

Stuart Robinson meets us in the foyer and leads us through another set of doors into the garden, where it seems as though we've left Skid Row altogether. The patio is an oasis of trees and benches, a manicured lawn and bougainvillea cascading over a wooden arbor. For the first time I can recall on Skid Row, birds are singing.

"Do you see that sign?" I ask Nathaniel as we stroll over to the arbor.

"No Smoking," he says enthusiastically.

This couldn't be more perfect. The few people who traipse through the garden are clients who live here in recovery from a combination of mental illness and drug or alcohol addiction. They carry themselves as if they're on the way up, with places to go, things to do. Lamp leases several apartments here and assigns a monitor to its residents, who have access to all of Lamp's services, from job training to psychiatric counseling and basic life management.

Judging by Nathaniel's reaction, he's not quite as jazzed as I am. He's still holding back, and I'm reluctant to push the matter by suggesting that we go see the room. I spot an empty bench and tell him it looks like a nice place to serenade passersby.

While Nathaniel tunes his cello, Robinson leads me down a ground-floor hallway to the room. Just inside the door is a closet and a vanity. On the right is the toilet and a shower stall. Straight ahead is a single carpeted room about twelve feet square, with a window onto the courtyard. It's small and modest, nothing special about it except that it could be the place where, for the first time in many years, Nathaniel makes a home.

Back in the garden, he has a small audience. I look up to see a woman in a second-floor apartment slide her window open so she can hear the concert, and she smiles down at me.

"*Nathaniel, that sounded great.* Would you like to take a break now and see the apartment?"

"I'm not interested in that."

"That's fine. But Mr. Snyder is probably going to want to check it out." I'm struggling for something else to use on him and find my answer in a cloudy sky. "Besides, it could rain on the day of your lesson and you'll have no choice but to go inside."

He agrees to have a look, but only after reloading his cart, which takes another fifteen minutes. Down the hall we go, him pushing the buggy, me worrying it's not going to fit through the door. That would be the end of it.

He begins wedging and angling the cart.

"How about if I—"

"No, no," he says. "Let me get all of that."

He unhooks the buckets, a boot, a giant squirt gun and a few other scraps that hang over the side. He pivots, grunts and pushes, and by divine intervention, the cart squeezes into the room. I celebrate silently. And Nathaniel? He drops to the floor to inspect the cigarette burns in the carpet.

"Looks like someone might have dropped a candle there," I say. Lying has become frightfully easy.

"I don't like it in here," he says.

"That's because it's too dark and stuffy," I answer, opening the blinds and cracking the window. An oleander scratches at the screen.

"Look at that," I say. "Plenty of light. It's like being in the garden."

He wonders why he can't take lessons at Disney Hall, or better yet, the tunnel.

"People will come in through that door and steal everything you've got," he says, looking as though he might cry. "I'm not ever going to be in here again, and I don't care about that Snyder thing, János Starker, Walt Disney Concert Hall, Donald Duck, *Fantasia*. I don't need any of that."

It's his nature to resist, to always do things his way. I wonder, though, if the issue isn't lack of desire but fear of change. I walk over to the window and sniff the flowers outside. One of the twin beds is on its side against a wall, and I tell him that leaves a convenient space for his shopping cart.

"The place has a nice feel," I say. "I wonder what the acoustics are like in here."

Nathaniel reaches for his cello. Slowly. Reluctantly. He sits on the edge of the bed and plays Schubert's Arpeggione. The music surrounds us, and he closes his eyes.

16

The kids stood weeping at the airport window in Cleveland as the plane pulled away from the gate. Their father waved from his window seat, and Nathaniel remained silent as the plane taxied away and took off for California.

It was 1962. He was eleven years old and didn't understand any of it.

"Why can't I go?" he asked.

There had been signs of trouble. His father smashing a phone down on the floor the night his mother said she had to work at a fashion show. The Sunday ride to church when Jennifer got bumped to the backseat to make room for her father's lady friend. But Nathaniel was too young to give meaning to any of that. Through the eyes of an eleven-year-old, things could not have been better.

His dad worked at the Willard battery company and his mother ran Floria's Beauty Lounge on St. Clair, primping the women whose husbands worked in the factories that had fed the city's children for decades. The salon was a short walk from the two-story family home at East Ninety-fifth and Seminole, and Nathaniel darted in and out of his mother's shop, did homework there and was happy to charm her customers with his wide-eyed chatter and proper manners. Flo's boy had character and poise, and he easily fell under the spell of the music his mother played on an old RCA radio. Whether it was jazz standards, classical or pop, the mellow sounds that filled the shop would sometimes put the youngster in a trance.

Mr. and Mrs. Ayers were never flush with cash, but they did just fine and believed a proper upbringing should include exposure to the arts, especially in a city that could boast one of the great orchestras of the world and a grand performance hall situated on nearby University Circle. The Ayers family bought an upright piano for their living room and arranged for Del and Nathaniel to have lessons with a Mrs. Lockhart, and it became apparent, as Nathaniel worked through the John Thompson piano course books, that their son seemed to have a good ear and nimble fingers.

But Nathaniel was too busy to get very good at it. When the hard Cleveland winters would thaw and the gray city came back to life, Nathaniel ran over to his uncle Howard and aunt Willa's house on East 111th because they lived across the street from a park. Nathaniel played football with neighborhood kids and chipped golf balls with Uncle Howard, who topped six feet and seemed a giant to Nathaniel. If there was nothing doing in the park, Nathaniel scooted over to the lake to gaze at the steaming tankers, check out the activity on the docks or chuck stones into the lapping surf. When he charged along the shore he was Jim Brown of the Cleveland Browns. When he cocked his arm and let a stone fly across Lake Erie, he was Mudcat Grant of the Indians. He listened to ball games on his transistor radio and read about them the next day in the *Plain Dealer*. How could his parents not be happy together when life was so full and there was so much fun to be had in Cleveland? How could his father be moving out, and who would ever take him to an Indians game?

Nathaniel was silent all the way home from the airport. When they got back to the house, he talked to no one and refused to play with Jennifer. He couldn't understand how his father could abandon the family, or why he had gone to a place so far away. Los Angeles? How could that be better than Cleveland?

Nathaniel became fixated on California, wanted to visit his father and was polite but indifferent toward the men who came calling on his mother about a year after the split. One in particular seemed to be coming around a lot, which didn't sit well with Nathaniel. Was he going to lose his mother now, too?

Get your things together, Floria Ayers told her children one day. They were moving a few miles away, into the home of her new husband. Nathaniel hadn't begun to digest the thought of leaving his house, his bedroom or his neighborhood when an even worse surprise was sprung on him. Alexander Mangrum, his new stepfather, had four children. Overnight, the Ayers kids went from being masters of their own home to sharing space with a house full of strangers who weren't exactly pleased to have them squeeze in. The house, at 10923 Churchill Avenue, was a two-story walk-up with a nice porch and good-size backyard, but Nathaniel's friends were too far away now, and so were the park and the lake. It felt as though his mother was gone now, too, because he had to fight for her attention. Why couldn't he go live with his father in Los Angeles? Here, he was a stepchild, and so were Del and Jennifer. They had to do something, Nathaniel insisted in a discreet huddle with his sisters.

But what?

"Let's run away," Nathaniel said. He'd always heard about kids running away from home but never understood why anyone would. Until now. His new stepbrothers didn't like him and he didn't much care for them, either.

Del was not unsympathetic. She was having just as hard a time adjusting as Nathaniel was. As the eldest, at fifteen, she had been very close to her mother and devastated by the upheaval of the past two years. But she was plainspoken and adultlike in her sense of responsibility, and she asked Nathaniel a question that had not occurred to him.

"Where are we going to go?"

Nathaniel had to think about it for a while, but he finally came up with a plan. They should grab their things in the dark of night, sneak down the stairs and hightail it to Uncle Howard and Aunt Willa's house.

"And you don't think they're going to call our mother the minute we get there?" Delsinia asked.

Nathaniel hadn't thought of that. His big sister was right. They were stuck, and Nathaniel's confidence and outgoing personality slowly began to fade. He broke down and cried, humiliated, when his stepbrothers got the best of him in a backyard push-up contest, and his sisters saw him sink even deeper after a much-anticipated trip to California. His father's new wife and stepchildren were as foreign to him as the crowd in the house on Churchill Street, and Nathaniel felt there was no room for him in his father's life. The young man returned to Cleveland more sullen, more broken and yet more grown-up, it seemed. His despair gradually evolved into the source of his resolve, and as the boy became the young man, he noticed that his stepsisters were suddenly showing more interest in him. Nathaniel began impeccably grooming himself before setting foot outside the house, and the stepsisters cooed as he worked the mirror, and them. The hair just so. The sweater snug over the shoulders, emphasizing the biceps. He was cute and smart, and the personality was coming back. Maybe things wouldn't be so bad, after all, in this new life on Churchill Street. One advantage, he was about to discover, was that just down the street, a junior high teacher and longtime musician was rebuilding the school band program and looking for talent.

William Moon had been handpicked by the principal of Harry E. Davis Jr. High School. The principal knew Moon as a good teacher and bona fide musician who had played trombone in Cleveland's lauded all-black Navy band, an association that came into being because of segregation, so he lured Moon from another public school. This was a time when music was considered essential in the education of an American child, and that was particularly so in Cleveland, where the fortunes amassed by the barons of industry had built Severance Hall and other great music institutions.

Moon, who lived on the east side with his wife and three children, not far from Nathaniel's uncle Howard and aunt Willa, was a patient man. How else would he survive each day among adolescents, many of whom had never held an instrument in their hands and were hearing classical tunes for the first time? Moon taught beginning basics, encouraged students to grab any instrument that struck their fancy and gradually pushed them toward learning the scales. His love of music got him through such trials, and so did the fact that there were one or two students who had both a knack and a desire.

Nathaniel? Was that the name of the boy with the strong, elegant hands? The one who didn't appear intimidated by any of the instruments or the dreaded dry recitation of music theory? The young man seemed rather astute, Moon thought, and determined, as well. Moon pegged him to play one of his own favorite instruments—the sousaphone.

Nathaniel was an A's and B's student, articulate, respectful and polite. He said Mister and Misses and rounded his O's in a refined Midwestern way, but he was not about to wrap that brass pipe up around his head and over his shoulders like a pet python.

"No, thank you," he said. "No, thank you, sir."

Mr. Moon explained that the sousaphone was a traditional instrument in African-American bands, but Nathaniel wasn't persuaded. He was intrigued by several other instruments and interested more in the idea of music than any one discipline. He liked trumpet, and flute, and piano, and he especially liked the strings. Whatever he picked up, he was one of Mr. Moon's better musicians and a definite candidate for the school orchestra.

Mr. Moon, as it happened, had a daughter named Marjorie who was studying music on scholarship at Ohio University, where she played string bass. Moon was proud of her as both a musician and a gender-busting pioneer. At the time, music was primarily a boys' club. The Cleveland Orchestra, in fact, was all male. At Harry E. Davis, Moon wanted to encourage African-American girls, in particular, to take up music, and he thought his daughter's accomplished playing would inspire them. So when Marjorie was on break from Ohio U, Moon always arranged for her to come play in front of his students.

On one occasion, though, it wasn't one of Mr. Moon's female students who got taken in. It was a skinny young man who liked the idea of an instrument so tall you had to stand up and wrap your arms around it, an instrument that spoke in a deep and powerful voice you could feel coming up through the floorboards. Nathaniel Anthony Ayers, all of thirteen years old, was mesmerized by this instrument the size of a good strong man.

"That's what I want to do," Nathaniel told Mr. Moon, ending for good the teacher's sousaphone dreams. "I want to do what she does."

Marjorie Moon would wonder in the months to come, as her father enthusiastically updated her regarding his prize student's progress on the school's beat-up string bass, if there was another reason he had chosen that instrument.

"Does he have a father?" she asked her dad.

Mr. Moon didn't know the full details of Nathaniel's life, but wondered why his daughter would ask such a question.

It just struck her, Marjorie told her father, that maybe Nathaniel wanted to make Mr. Moon as proud of him as he was of his own daughter.

For the first time since his father had left, Nathaniel was alive, and he would race home from school to tell his family about band practice. Mr. Moon, determined to encourage the youngster, called Nathaniel's mother to tell her how delighted he was at how quickly Nathaniel was catching on to scales, rhythm and music theory. He's got a gift, Mr. Moon told her, and she would be wise to nurture it. Nathaniel's mother wasn't surprised, given the weekly piano lessons Nathaniel had taken for a couple of years along with his sister, Del. When she got the call from Mr. Moon, Floria called her son downstairs to tell him about it.

"So you like music?" she asked proudly.

"Yeah," said Nathaniel. "I do."

When his mother bought him a used bass, Nathaniel began passing up ball games in the street and in the schoolyard so he could practice. He was becoming so good that Mr. Moon couldn't help him any longer. Fortunately, Moon knew exactly whom to call about his star pupil. His daughter Marjorie had studied at a celebrated institution called the Cleveland Music School Settlement, where her teacher was a bass player from the famed Cleveland Orchestra.

Nathaniel could make the walk to the Music School Settlement from his home on the edge of the Glenville District in under thirty minutes. The Settlement, as he would come to call it, was situated in the most enchanted neighborhood in all of Cleveland. University Circle, named for the turnaround of the Euclid Avenue trolley from downtown, was home to Case Western Reserve University, the Cleveland Museum of Art, the Cleveland Institute of Music and the jewel of the neighborhood—Severance Hall. The Georgian-style home of the Cleveland Orchestra—financed by John Long Severance, the son of John D. Rockefeller's treasurer— was hailed as an architectural triumph and had hosted its first concert in 1931, with conductor Nikolai Sokoloff leading a program that included Bach's Passacaglia and Brahms's First Symphony. By the time Nathaniel strode by on the way to his first music lesson, the Cleveland Orchestra had become, under music director George Szell, one of the greatest ensembles in the world, and no one was prouder to be a part of it than Harry Barnoff. He was a stubby-fingered son of working-class Cleveland—his father was a maintenance man and his mother a sales clerk at the May Company, and his Hungarian-born mother's strudel brought a smile to the face of Szell, who was raised in Budapest.

One thing Barnoff had in common with Nathaniel was that there had been no musicians in his family's recent history. He had found his own way, exposed first through the radio in his parents' home, and later in band class at public schools in Cleveland, just like Nathaniel. He became serious in high school, later studied at Ohio University, and then won a scholarship to Juilliard. When he joined his hometown orchestra in 1960, Barnoff was determined to help younger students follow in his footsteps. This led to a job at the Cleveland Institute of Music, the more prestigious of the two schools on University Circle, but a friend talked him into considering an opening at the Settlement, which was literally a stone's throw away.

"It was less pay, but it was a red-feather institution," Barnoff says. "They took in everybody regardless of ability to pay, and I thought I could make a bigger difference there."

That was the very mission at the Settlement, a nonprofit that had opened its doors in 1912 to people of all ages and all musical abilities. Music was too beautiful and powerful a force to be embraced by only a select few, believed Almeda Adams. Adams, born in Pennsylvania and blind from the age of six months, had studied piano and voice at the New England Conservatory of Music and later settled with her family in Ohio. It was in Cleveland that her father read her an article about a music "settlement" in New York and pronounced, "You must do that thing for Cleveland. There is your work."

Adams went to New York to learn how it had been done, then returned to Cleveland to meet with an influential civic organization called the Fortnightly Musical Club. Cleveland was awash in money at the time, and certainly some of it could be used to foster the full development of the city's neediest inhabitants. This was the charge Adams took to Adella Prentiss Hughes, a prominent Fortnightly member who had been a promoter of the Metropolitan Opera, the Diaghilev Ballets Russes, and orchestras conducted by Gustav Mahler, Leopold Stokowski and Richard Strauss.

And so it began. By 1938, having already outgrown its quarters on East Ninety-third Street, the school used budding support from Cleveland high society to buy at a nominal fee a forty-two-room English manor on Magnolia Street in University Circle. When Nathaniel arrived in 1964, thousands of students had already passed through what had become one of the nation's largest community music schools. Built in 1910, it resembled a great country retreat or elegant hotel, with a sweeping cobblestone driveway. Nathaniel arrived to music wafting from the windows and mingling with the rustling of leaves on the shady estate. Once inside the building, he walked under carved ceilings and crystal chandeliers and past marble fireplaces. The place felt ancient and rich, with dark wood carvings and floors that creaked, sending echoes through a maze of hallways that had been walked by great musicians. Nathaniel descended a circular staircase to the basement, then walked down a long hall and into a carpeted space with one belowground window that threw scant light into the room.

Over the next several years, that dark chamber would become his sanctuary while the world outside changed. Industry, the lifeblood of Cleveland, was dying off and the signs included shuttered storefronts and weeds in the cracks of sidewalks. Crime was up, along with anger, hatred and resentment, and the sacrifice of local blood in the disastrous Vietnam War further split the city and the nation. Cleveland grew more divided by color and class, and both before and after the assassination of Martin Luther King, Nathaniel's general neighborhood—Cleveland's east side— was the scene of rioting, shoot-outs, looting, tear gas and firebombs. Harry Barnoff would see smoldering ruins in the distance as he drove to the Settlement, where he would always find his student at work in the basement. As Cleveland burned, Nathaniel, a black teenager with a white mentor, was hard at work on Beethoven and Brahms. If he kept at it, Barnoff told him, a music scholarship to Ohio University wasn't out of the question. Maybe, Nathaniel told him. But he had even bigger dreams than that. Hadn't Mr. Barnoff been to Juilliard?

17

Pete Snyder steps jauntily through the door of the Disney Hall lobby with a wave and a smile. He puts his cello in the backseat and gives me a firm handshake, looking natty in a light olive-colored leather jacket, his salt-and-pepper mustache freshly trimmed.

"I'm very excited about this," he says. "And a little bit nervous. I don't really know what to expect."

Snyder is Brooklyn-born and was raised in Los Angeles by two professional pianists of Russian and Romanian descent, and his mother had been his accompanist for his European debut in Vienna in 1966. He taught at two universities and joined the Pittsburgh Symphony in 1969 and the Los Angeles Philharmonic in 1973, but music is only one of his pursuits. Snyder studied animation, once published a comic strip and dabbles in sculpture. As far as he can determine, he tells me, there have been musicians and artists in every generation of his family dating back to at least 1800.

I note the irony of my being introduced to so rarefied an artistic community by a homeless man, reminding Snyder that I don't know classical music and can't judge Nathaniel's ability on cello. Snyder says it doesn't matter how well Nathaniel plays. He's hoping to be able to help him find his way. "I've given this a great deal of thought," he says. "I must say that he made a very deep impression on me."

Nathaniel is waiting for us in the courtyard of the Ballington. He nervously greets Snyder, taking two steps back, just as he did on my first encounter with him almost a year earlier. I suggest we move quickly into the apartment so as to get the most out of Mr. Snyder's visit, and Nathaniel raises no objection. So far, everything is working as planned.

"When did you last have a lesson?" I ask after Nathaniel has once again managed the engineering feat of squeezing his cart through the doorway.

He answers while breaking down the buggy, carefully moving a blue tarp and a white sheet that cover his cello and two violins. It had to be in the early 1970s, he says. It was right before a concert in Aspen.

"Did you play in Aspen?" Snyder asks.

"Yes, but I got into trouble with the psychiatrists there," Nathaniel says. "Straitjacket," he adds without further comment.

Snyder looks for my reaction, and all I've got for him is a shrug.

There's nothing in the room but a sheetless twin mattress and a dresser. I drag a couple of patio chairs in from the communal kitchen down the hall. Nathaniel and Mr. Snyder, as he calls him, are carrying on about musicians and music directors who were regulars at Aspen in the seventies.

"I brought you something," Snyder says, handing him the music to Pablo Casals's "Song of the Birds." "It's something appropriate, because you're kind of a wandering bird."

Nathaniel acknowledges the gift, but he's not quite with us. He grows distant and looks confused. It's as if a storm is moving through his head, tossing things around.

"I'm playing in the tunnels," he tells Snyder, "where Don Quixote and Colonel Sanders have been involved in a bloody battle."

If Snyder thought this was going to be easy, he now has reason to believe otherwise. But the cellist has come to this task with an open mind and more than a little confidence.

"That's a nice story," he says kindly, asking Nathaniel if he wouldn't mind having the cello tuned and ready to go at his next lesson, so they waste no time. Nathaniel gives off the slightest hint of an objection, but maybe this is just what he needs—a firm but supportive tutor. Despite his earlier confession, Snyder doesn't seem at all nervous now. If anyone's nervous, it is I. I want this to work. We couldn't have been luckier than to have a member of the orchestra volunteer his time to a homeless man who is mentally ill, selflessly trying to help in Nathaniel's recovery. And willing to come to Skid Row for the lesson.

Nathaniel begins playing without prompting the moment he's in tune. He does a little finger-dance sprint that nearly works him into a sweat, and his vibrato brings a smile to Snyder's face.

"You know, you're a very natural player," Snyder says, drawing a bashful shrug out of Nathaniel. Snyder tells him he likes his left-hand position, but he needs some work with his bowing. Nathaniel seems hungry for the feedback. It's been years since anyone as accomplished as Snyder has taken any time with him. Snyder, it's clear, has been touched by Nathaniel, as were so many teachers before him. I wonder, though, how much time Snyder has, and how much patience.

Harry Barnoff took Nathaniel's collect calls from the Aspen Music Festival and from mental hospitals in Cleveland. They were always the same. Nathaniel was manic, paranoid, confused. He needed to hear a familiar voice, and Barnoff would try to calm him by asking about the music he was playing. Homer Mensch, Nathaniel's first teacher at Juilliard, once called the police to his home across the street from Juilliard. Nathaniel was rambling in a delusional, menacing way.

Gary Karr was Nathaniel's next teacher. A legend among bass players and only a few years older than Nathaniel, the Juilliard grad was one of the few bass players in the world good enough to build a career as a soloist. Karr had studied under Stuart Sankey in Aspen, just as Nathaniel had. He also had been a featured soloist, at the age of twenty, in a nationally televised performance of the New York Philharmonic Young People's Concert. With Leonard Bernstein conducting, Karr played "The Swan" from Saint-Saëns's *Carnival of the Animals*.

In Nathaniel, Karr saw great promise and little discipline.

He'd assign him a piece to learn, and Nathaniel would return without having taken it seriously. Instead, he'd show Karr something else he'd been pouring his heart into, and whatever it was from one week to the next, it was good enough that Karr would let him slide. If Karr was partial to his fellow bass player, it was partly because of lingering resentment over his own experience as a Juilliard student. A star system was in place, as he saw it, and it worked to the detriment of a majority of students. Violinists, pianists, cellists—those were the quarterbacks on the Juilliard team. The bass players were like lumbering offensive linemen, clearing the way for the stars to shine. And yet they faced the same unbearable pressure to excel. But Karr says Nathaniel had bigger problems than that.

"He seemed to be struggling with his racial identity in a nearly all-white environment," recalls Karr, who himself was aware of a growing racial division in the professional community of musicians. African-Americans, particularly in jazz, were speaking up after years of getting shafted on record deals and banishment from the hotels where white colleagues stayed. Karr was empathetic, but also disappointed in black jazz musicians who were giving him the cold shoulder after years of friendship. He wanted badly to make his relationship with Nathaniel work for both of them.

"He had a way. Anyone who came into a room would be drawn to him. He had a kind of charisma, and it being the seventies, I don't recall many black students, so he kind of stuck out."

When Nathaniel flubbed assignments, Karr directed him to more work by Ernest Bloch, whose music he considered soul explorations. Maybe Nathaniel would find himself in Bloch's inspired expressions.

"His sound was very good. He was a natural talent and there was always real passion. I think most of what he learned at Juilliard was from his own instincts rather than anything I or anyone else taught him. I found him really hard to reach. He marched to his own drummer, always."

At about this time, Karr noticed that New York's population of addled street dwellers was exploding. Mental hospitals were emptied and with too few clinics to manage their problems, many former patients ended up squatting in subway stations, on street corners and in Central Park. Mental illness was on public display, and in the army of lost souls, Karr saw some of the same anger and disorientation he was seeing in Nathaniel. As the school year progressed, Nathaniel's problems became more pronounced, and Karr began to suspect that the hostility he had attributed to race had an entirely different origin. Was it even safe to set foot in a room with Nathaniel, one-on-one? Karr wondered. Nathaniel would occasionally erupt, commandeering the conversation and driving it from music to racial injustice. He insisted Karr had no way of appreciating the black experience. At times, his tone was threatening. He trembled and seemed on the verge of coming unraveled.

"I said something to him like, 'Hey, man.' He said, 'Don't you ever call me Hey Man.' I remember walking on glass with him. I was so guarded. I remember he raised his hand up like he was ready to strike. I don't remember what I said to back him off, but he got something in his head and I think he was going to strike me. I went to the administration and said, 'You know, this guy has problems.' And I was not going to continue giving him lessons without someone else in the room."

Karr said the administration blew off his suggestion that Nathaniel had a mental condition, suggesting instead that his problem was racially motivated attitude.

"Since I'm not a specialist on mental disorders, they refused to acknowledge my recommendations that he seek psychiatric help. Instead of dealing with his personal problem, he seemed to be lumped into the category of a typically angry African-American, although I didn't see it that way. In Nathaniel's case, I knew that something was dreadfully wrong."

"Do you know this?" Snyder asks, playing his own cello to show Nathaniel the way.

"Bach Bourrée in C major," says Nathaniel.

Snyder nods and continues playing, and I realize for the first time how far Nathaniel has to go. Snyder's playing is polished and complete, with none of the tangled thoughts and lost threads I've become accustomed to in Nathaniel's music. Snyder is the instrument's master rather than the reverse. The biggest difference is the pitch and pace of the music, and Nathaniel sits in a trance, his mouth open as he watches. He's particularly focused on the fingering, leaning in for closer study, then falls back and I can't tell whether he's inspired or destroyed. But when Snyder asks if he'd like to take a pass at the Bouree, Nathaniel doesn't hesitate.

He stops and starts, apologizes, gives it another try and keeps on. His sound is harsher than Snyder's, with too much vibration and the occasional squeal. It's impossible for me to know whether this is because of an inferior instrument or because Nathaniel was trained on bass rather than cello. Or whether his illness limits his ability. But he begins to smooth things out as he continues, even if his motion appears more labored after Snyder's fluid strokes. His sound mellows in time, with Snyder encouraging him to lengthen his strokes and keep up the rhythm. He plays with more confidence now and becomes more animated, working the vibrato with a flourish.

I look to Snyder for an assessment.

"I'm amazed," he says.

I feel like a parent whose child has just aced his audition.

"I know many talented people who don't have as pretty a sound," Snyder says.

Gary Karr said the same. If you put your very existence into it, your sensitivity and humanity, it makes for a sound distinctly yours, Karr told me. Nathaniel plays music that silences the voices in his head. It's proof his illness hasn't touched his soul.

Snyder leans into me as Nathaniel plays on.

"He might be a musical genius. It's not unusual to find someone with his aptitude. What is unbelievable is to see someone without recent training play so well."

Snyder tells Nathaniel this is a great start, and if he's willing to work at it, this could be the first of many lessons in this room.

That's all it takes, one sour note, and the other Nathaniel resurfaces.

"It's not my room," he says in a smart tone. "I'm not going to be living in here."

But why not? Snyder asks. It makes perfect sense to have a quiet place to practice.

"You have a gift, and you need to respect it and be grateful to

God for granting it," Snyder says, adding that he can build his spiritual strength through music.

Nathaniel nods but is obviously annoyed. He hadn't expected the lesson to include a sermon. He tells Snyder he's more comfortable in the tunnel or out by the Beethoven statue.

"Every criminal in Los Angeles will be coming through that door right there and they will steal everything I've got. That's how the drug addict operates. He will steal and steal and steal to support his habit, and I am not going to be in here with all my things so they can just come in here and take whatever they want."

He hasn't completely lost it yet, but he's headed in that direction. I'm about to step in before it escalates, but Snyder responds before I do.

"How about making this deal," he says. "You come here as often as you can, so maybe we can have another lesson."

Nathaniel is back to his mantra. There's no one to deal with in the tunnel, no one to bother him. And the sound is better there, too. In the tunnel, he hears the city all around and doesn't feel cut off from it like he does inside these four walls.

Snyder isn't giving any ground. He leans in close and says: "Think of this as a clean, quiet tunnel."

Nathaniel is at least giving it some consideration.

"I wouldn't have thought of it," he says. "Yeah. This is a brand-new tunnel."

18

The Country Club Apartments for Seniors is a modern two-story affair near Charleston and Valley View Road in Las Vegas, a few miles northwest of the famous Strip. The elder Nathaniel Ayers lives there in retirement from his job as a trash truck driver in Los Angeles. He fills his days with Bible readings and trips to Mountaintop Faith, his house of worship. Mr. Ayers's son never speaks ill of him, despite the long years that go by without contact. I've come to Las Vegas not because I want to get to know Mr. Ayers, but because I'm trying to better understand his son.

Mr. Ayers's stepdaughter has agreed to make an introduction, telling me he's hard of hearing and doesn't pick up the phone. But when I land in Las Vegas and drive to the apartments, she doesn't answer my call. I try several times and finally get her. She's forgotten about my visit and is in Palm Springs for a quick getaway.

I've come too far to give up that easily, so I walk into the apartment house lobby to see if anyone can tell me where to find Mr. Ayers. Several people are watching the clubhouse TV or reading, but they've never heard of any Mr. Ayers. In the office I find a clerk who says she's new and doesn't know many of the residents. My last hope is the pool area, where several folks are taking some sun. On my way there, I see a Bible on a coffee table, and a name is written on the edge of it.

"Nathaniel Ayers."

I scoop up the *Miracle Breakthrough Bible* and open it to the ribbon marker, which is at Chronicles 2. I find no address in the book, so I go back to the office to announce that Mr. Ayers seems to have forgotten his Bible in the clubhouse and would probably like to have it back. If there's any way she could do a little snooping and dig up his apartment number, I'll personally deliver the Bible to him as a friend of his son, so he doesn't have to be without. This gets me through the gates.

Mr. Ayers has a first-floor unit not far from the pool, and as I walk to it I hear Jennifer's voice in my head, bristling at how little her father did to make his children feel welcome in his new life. She's particularly angry about the way he ignored his troubled son. Jennifer's mother married twice more after Mr. Ayers left her for California, and the third one was the charm. He was more of a father to Nathaniel than his biological father had been, but Nathaniel didn't necessarily look at it that way. His real father was the one whose affection he most coveted.

I stand at the door and peer through the screen. Mr. Ayers is asleep on a chair in the living room, sitting no more than four feet from a television with the volume blasting. I call out and bang on the screen door, but he doesn't stir. I bang louder and he finally picks himself up and stiff-legs his way to the door, bent over by a bad back.

There's no doubt this is Nathaniel's father. His skin is lighter, but the features are the same. Flat nose, hooded eyes, shiny white teeth built into a slightly protuberant mouth. Like his son, the elder Ayers has a long thin trunk built atop a body that's broader from the waist down.

I hold up his Bible and announce myself, then again, and again, louder each time, until every resident of the Country Club Apartments knows that Steve Lopez, his son's friend from Los Angeles, has arrived to interview him for a book about Nathaniel.

Finally he catches on. He's heard about me but wasn't expecting me.

Mr. Ayers invites me in and lowers himself back into his armchair. He's frail and so hard of hearing he has no idea the television is loud enough to shake quarters out of the slots on the Strip. I point to the TV and to my ear. He gets the message and turns it down. I hand him his Bible and as he takes hold of it I see Nathaniel's fingers, slender and elegant. No, Mr. Ayers says, he never picked up an instrument.

"After I came out of the army, he was born," Mr. Ayers says of Nathaniel. "And the two sisters. And then we broke up."

That's always tough on everyone, I say.

"She put me out," he says.

Why?

"I guess I'm a bad fella."

Really?

"Nah, I'm just tellin' you that."

Jennifer tells a different story. She says he wanted an old-fashioned woman, not a successful and gregarious entrepreneur like her mother, Flo. Jennifer recalls a night when her mother announced she had to work at a beauty show and Mr. Ayers told her she had more important work at home. They stared each other down until Mrs. Ayers grabbed her coat and hat and stomped off to work. Jennifer also tells a story about their trips to church on Sunday. She would ride up front because their mother wasn't churchgoing, and they'd stop along the way to pick up a neighbor lady. Jennifer remembers vividly the day they stopped at the neighbor's house and her father ordered her into the backseat so the lady could sit up front. That was the lady he later married, and they moved to California.

I'm sure Mr. Ayers might have a different take on the particulars, but I haven't come to delve further into any of that. I tell him about my friendship with his son and my efforts to help him build a better life for himself.

Mr. Ayers sniffs at the suggestion.

"I think he likes doing just what he's doing," he says flatly. "Being around unfortunate people."

I swallow back my anger. It's such a harsh and uninformed comment, I don't even know how to begin to respond. His own father has written Nathaniel off as a man who has chosen the life he lives. Not that Jennifer didn't warn me. Her father never was understanding or sensitive on this issue, she said.

I ask Mr. Ayers, as kindly as I can, if he is aware that his son is mentally ill. I have to shout this more than once. The father who walked out on a son who lives for music has been robbed of his hearing, and there has to be a Sunday sermon in that.

"The first I knew of it he was in school in New York City. Juilliard. I don't know. He played bass and somebody may have slipped something into his drink. He knew all the police officers in Cleveland, so they wouldn't lock him up."

Maybe I have no business asking the next question, but I can't help myself.

"Do I miss him?" Mr. Ayers repeats. "Well, I haven't had too much time to miss him. What bothered me most was we didn't get along too good, you know? He sometimes, I think he'd just do things to aggravate me. So many things have happened that's beyond my comprehension. I can't understand it. He fell out with his mother because she divorced me. I honestly believe that he gave her a hard time in the last years of her life."

I don't know why I continue. Maybe just because I've gone to the trouble of flying to Las Vegas to meet the man Nathaniel still calls "my father" and still occasionally expresses an interest in seeing. But his father is a man who doesn't know him.

"One Christmas, it was eighty degrees. He came to see me in California and turned around and went back early, after I had paid for him to come. He said it was too warm. He came other times, too. Sometimes he was all right, but he's kind of mixed up. I think he cared for me, but he had a funny way of showing it. He was on prescription drugs. They tried to keep his nerves down with drugs and I don't believe in that. That's what messed him up the most. Prescription drugs."

I'm nodding agreeably at this point. It's obvious there's no point in my responding.

"I think about him all the time," Mr. Ayers says. "I'll never forget him. I'm praying for him night and day, every time I think about it. I remember having a picture of him. I don't remember where it is."

He's a talented man, I say, telling Mr. Ayers that winning a scholarship to Juilliard is rare. Had Mr. Ayers ever heard his son play? I ask.

"One Christmas we had a little party and he played 'Silent Night,'" he says. "I don't remember the other songs he played."

It's a shame, Mr. Ayers says, that his son has thrown away his talent and his life.

"I got to where I felt he understood what he was doing and didn't have to do it. What's wrong with him? I don't know how to explain it. I don't think nothing's wrong with his brain. It's the prescription drugs mostly."

Is Mr. Ayers completely unaware that his son was diagnosed with a very specific disease?

"He mentioned something to me about schizophrenia, I think they call it. I don't know nothing much about that kind of thing. The way it happened, I didn't get a chance to feel bad about it because everything worked out well for my children."

It's clear now that it's time for me to go. I'm not sure why I do it, but I tell Mr. Ayers his son misses him and I ask if he has anything he'd like me to pass along to Nathaniel or Jennifer and Del.

"Tell him I miss all of them. I'm proud of all of them. There couldn't be no prouder a man than me of all his children."

. . .

Marjorie Moon was right all those many years ago about the young man who was trying so hard to win his teacher's attention. Nathaniel saw a proud glow on Mr. Moon's face the day Marjorie visited his class to play the bass, and he longed for a relationship with someone, particularly a man, who would feel the same way about him. For many years, Harry Barnoff was the man Nathaniel tried so hard to impress. It was Barnoff he called when he was in trouble, and it was Barnoff whose phone number he still had committed to memory more than twenty years after the last time he dialed it.

I'm the one he calls now, the one who, when it comes to music, is student rather than teacher. He calls me at work, calls me at home, calls me on my cell phone. Sometimes it's something specific he's after. He needs rosin or a new string, or he wonders if I can find a particular piece of sheet music for him. Other times it seems as though he calls just to know that I'm there. "Hello, Mr. Lopez," he always begins, asking about every member of my family.

After Las Vegas, I wonder if Nathaniel's success as a young musician was at least in part a cry for his father's notice, or perhaps a defiant message that Dad's abandonment had only made him stronger. A little of both, perhaps.

"I was in Las Vegas over the weekend," I tell Nathaniel two days after my return. "I met your father."

"How is he?" he asks, a little hurt that I didn't take him with me. We had talked about Nathaniel visiting him at some point, but I wasn't sure the time was right yet.

"He's fine, but getting old."

I tell Nathaniel I filled his father in on how he's doing. He asks what his father said in response.

"He told me he misses you," I say. "And he couldn't be any prouder."

19

———✦———

Stuart Robinson got into the wrong business after college. He assembled parts for military aircraft, which paid well but didn't do much for his soul, so getting laid off during a slowdown was a blessing. Robinson, who had studied psychology in college, took a job as a mental health counselor. Assembling lives felt more rewarding than his old job, and Robinson liked his new line of work well enough to go after an even bigger challenge. The Los Angeles Men's Project, which had a reputation for taking on the toughest cases, had an opening at its San Julian site, and Robinson got the job.

I've seen him escort screaming troublemakers off the premises, talk police out of arresting a client for jaywalking, talk down a man threatening suicide, give aid to a stabbing victim and calmly tell a certain musician to stop flipping out every time he sees someone smoking cigarettes. It's common, in fact, for all of that and more to be going on at the same time. It helps, for the sake of intimidation, that Robinson is the size of an NFL lineman. He also has a surprisingly soft voice for such a hulking presence, which makes for a calming counterbalance to the three-ring madness that surrounds him. Madness that is now frequently set to music, thanks to Nathaniel.

In a courtyard full of characters, Nathaniel is second to none. If he's not trying to figure out the Bach Unaccompanied Cello Suites, he's drawing on the pavement with a rock, writing the name of whatever piece he's playing, the name of the composer, Peter Snyder, Adam Crane, Governor Schwarzenegger, the names of me and everyone in my family or whatever else pops into his head. He has also taken it upon himself to expand his janitorial services beyond the retrieval of cigarette butts. Now he often sweeps, mops, takes out the trash and seems to be in competition with the actual janitor.

"He does want to give back," Robinson says, and it's no small development. Nathaniel's desire to pitch in is a sign of his growing comfort with Lamp and with Robinson. He sees himself as part of a community now, and because he values what's being done for him, he wants to show his appreciation and sense of responsibility.

I know I'm not supposed to keep asking, especially since the question has no answer. But I need to know if Robinson thinks we're getting close.

"We could be," he says. "But he's still got a few things to work out."

"Like what?"

Robinson pauses to think about it.

Sometimes, he says, it's not that clients don't want to move inside. It's that they don't trust their own ability to hold on to a place of their own, or they fear that something or someone will force them out. The advantage to life on the street, Robinson says, is that you have nothing to lose.

A week after the lesson with Pete Snyder, Nathaniel approaches Robinson with a question. Can he please park his buggy in the apartment while he goes to look for some sheet music at the library?

Robinson calls me, excited about the news. To him, a little thing like this isn't such a little thing. It's a promising break-through. Nathaniel is confronting his fears and thinking more rationally. Yes, it's actually true that someone might break into his room and steal everything he owns. But that's not likely to happen, he has concluded, so it's worth the risk.

Robinson happily escorted Nathaniel to the room and let him hear the turning of the lock when they left. Nathaniel was gone for a few hours, went to find Robinson again upon his return and discovered that the buggy had been untouched in the locked room.

This is all so encouraging, I'm determined to get Snyder back for another lesson right away to try to keep the momentum going. But it turns out the cellist is out of town for a few weeks.

Now what?

I don't know if there's any science to support my notion that momentum can be an important part of the recovery process, but it seems to make sense, and I haven't let my ignorance get in my

way before. Nathaniel hated the idea of coming to Lamp and now
he's a regular. He refused to set foot in the room and now he's
taken a lesson there and parked his cart there. The experts have
been telling me recovery is not always linear, but I'm a natural
skeptic and, besides, Nathaniel is making progress. Schizophren-
ics are creatures of habit, Dr. Ragins has told me. I'm determined
to make the room habit-forming, and I think I've got an idea
that's worth a try.

Nathaniel still insists he's going to pay me back one day for the
supplies and repairs. So I tell him I think I may have a way for
him to cover his debt.

"Have you ever taught music?" I ask as he heaves a big trash
bag into the dumpster at the Lamp courtyard.

No, he says.

"Because I think you'd make a good teacher," I say.

"Oh, I don't know about that."

"Well, I was wondering if you'd give me violin lessons."

I'm grateful he doesn't laugh. Look, I tell him, I was never
exposed to classical music before meeting him. Now I'm playing
it in my car and buying CDs, and I know I'd make for a fairly old
beginner, but why shouldn't I try to learn something new?

"Everyone can learn to play," he says. "I cannot understand
why Los Angeles is not coming to the Beethoven statue to find
inspiration from that man. Who put the statue there? Do you
know? It has to be there for a reason. I know that when I walked
through there and saw Beethoven, I knew I was in Los Angeles.
This is the Beethoven city."

"So will you give me lessons?"

"Sure," he says.

Now it's all going my way. A woman sitting alone on a bench in the Lamp courtyard is screaming like a televangelist in a yodeling contest.

"Well," I tell Nathaniel, "we can't do it here. Too noisy."

He couldn't be more annoyed by the noise. He looks at the woman and back at me, his eyes dizzy as he runs a finger in a circle around his ear. The sign for crazy.

Well, I guess it is all relative. I'd like to laugh but that doesn't seem appropriate. Instead I tell him I'm going to need some privacy for my lesson. A quiet place nearby, such as, say, his apartment.

Luckily, I step into the apartment before Nathaniel sees it. Just inside the doorway is a puddle of congealing blood.

"You know what?" I say, stepping back and pulling the door shut. "This is such a nice day, let's have the lesson in the courtyard."

The last thing I need is for Nathaniel to associate the apartment with what looked like the bloody remains of a human sacrifice. I call Stuart Robinson while Nathaniel sets up under the arbor and tell him it looks like something has died in the apartment. He says a Lamp client stayed there for a night or two and she's been sick, so maybe she vomited blood. It's still Nathaniel's room, he tells me, but he can't let it go to waste while other clients wait for housing. I'm in no position to argue the point. I can't expect Nathaniel to get a better deal than he's already got at Lamp, and this is a reminder that his privileges are not irrevocable. I've got to get him inside soon or it might not happen at all.

Robinson sends someone to clean the mess while I report for

the first violin lesson of my life. I've brought one of the five violins donated by readers—I've been carrying it around in the trunk of my car because two others were taking up all the space under my desk.

"This is mine?" Nathaniel asks when I hold it up for inspection.

"Yeah, along with your other five violins."

Nathaniel likes knowing he has them in reserve and double-checks every now and then to make sure I'm still holding on to them. He tunes this one and hands it back to me as if I know what to do with it. Just watch, he says, as he plays a little ditty on his violin and tells me to do the same on mine.

"Are you kidding? I don't even know how to hold this thing."

I wouldn't have expected it to feel so awkward in my hands, but the violin seems to have been designed for a smaller person, with fingers the size of gherkins. I am six foot two, with long digits, and everything feels too small and delicate to me. It doesn't help that the trick is to wedge the instrument at the curve of my neck and hold it there with my chin. Have I pulled a muscle already? My farsightedness is another issue. Straining at this odd angle, it's all a blur, and I could just as well be holding a red snapper.

Nathaniel takes the violin from me and tucks it under his chin in a way that looks perfectly natural.

"There, like that."

I give it another try, but with my shoulder humped to keep the instrument in place, I'm certain I must look like the Hunchback of Notre Dame.

"Like this?"

"Yes, now just do this," he says, striking a few notes.

I take up the bow, but don't know how to properly hold that, either. He gives me a quick demonstration, patient as a kindergarten teacher. I give it a whirl, but with bow to strings, I get a scratching noise that does not begin to resemble music.

Nathaniel takes a closer look and tells me the bow is the problem. It needs to be rehaired and coated with rosin.

"It's like feeding your parakeet," I say, stealing a line he uttered way back when I first met him.

He gives me one of his bows and I try again. This time the contact actually makes some detectable sounds, none of which can be called pleasant, and my instructor's interest seems to be waning. My first clue is that he has stopped watching, as if purposely averting his glance, and moved on to the cello.

"Come on, help me out here," I plead. I'm not expecting miracles, but neither did I imagine I'd feel this clumsy and inept. At the moment, the whole concept seems flawed. Getting the left and right hands to work together in such an awkward location was obviously someone's idea of a cruel joke centuries ago, and soft fingertips on hair-thin strings is uncomfortable enough that I'm ready to confess all my sins. The strings are also impossibly close together, so that fingering one without pawing others is a variation of pick-up sticks.

"There," Nathaniel says with encouragement. "You get a sound and work with it."

But the sound I've gotten is something a butcher hears while working with live chickens.

"It's frustrating," my teacher reassures, "but if you admire the violin, you'll weather the frustrations. Desire, discipline, diversity."

Perhaps, but no amount of desire, discipline or diversity can help me pick out the notes to "Twinkle, Twinkle, Little Star." A resident walks by and winces. While I struggle with a children's lullaby, Nathaniel breezes through Beethoven's Ninth to completely demoralize me. Several residents have come by to see what this is all about, but it's not me they care to watch. They're looking at the cellist with the white shirt tied around his head like a turban and the blue cardigan that has a tennis ball in one pocket and a dinner roll in the other. One of the spectators is carrying a battery-operated drill, and he begins gunning it in rhythm. *Bzzzzz. Bzzzzz. Bzzzzz.* Two of the others say they're musicians, and I suggest they start a band. The Ballington Five, or, if the guy with the drill sticks with them, the Black and Deckers. One man calls Nathaniel's music "dynamic" and hands him a dollar. All along, I'm hoping this spontaneous little festival will make Nathaniel feel more comfortable here.

When it's just the two of us I steer the conversation around to his mother, who got him started on those piano lessons when he was in primary school. Jennifer has told me that for all the suffering Nathaniel put his mother through, she was talking about him to Jennifer and Del at her last birthday in a nursing home. "I miss Anthony," she said while her only son was roaming the streets and, at that point, sleeping in the woods at times and carving on trees.

"You know," I tell him, "your mother would probably like to know you've got this. A nice little courtyard, some good neighbors and a place to lay your head if you ever get tired of the street and want to get at least one good night's sleep."

"I lost a god and I gained a god," Nathaniel says. "It's rough out there, but as long as I can look at Beethoven, I'll be all right."

Nathaniel lets me try his cello, which feels more comfortable than the violin. But this is sure to be another sad spectacle, and a man wanders over to see just how bad I'm willing to let myself look in public. He gets in pretty close, stands next to the "Smoking Prohibited" sign and lights a cigarette.

Nathaniel leaps into action.

"Excuse me, sir. You can't smoke here," he says with authority, as if someone has appointed him courtyard monitor.

"Who are you?" asks the man, who calls himself James. "You don't live here."

"I do, too, live here," Nathaniel insists. "I have a place."

Was it because I invoked his mother's memory? Was it because Stuart Robinson so cleverly and patiently planted the seed? Was it just time? Whatever the reasons, it's suddenly and finally looking as though there might be a payoff at the end of this year-long journey. I'm reluctant to let myself celebrate because it might never happen, but Nathaniel is standing his ground with James, insisting he's got a stake in the affairs of the Ballington.

"Where's your place?" James demands skeptically.

"Room B-116," Nathaniel says, pointing toward the window. "You're in violation of the city ordinance against smoking in that spot."

"Well, so what? I don't have a house on wheels."

It's a cruel schoolyard taunt, but Nathaniel is up to the challenge.

"You see," he says. "I knew it was personal."

"You need soap and water," says James.

"You're killing yourself and everyone else," Nathaniel retorts.

"Get a doctor. Get some help. You know what? It's a shame you allowed yourself to give up."

Now James has me ticked off. I'm tempted to step in and speak up for Nathaniel, but he has survived on his own for years and doesn't need me now.

"I didn't give up," he says.

"You're a young man, strong, you could get a job," James yammers. "You're a musician and you should encourage someone else. You can't encourage no one looking like that. Look at all that talent gone to waste."

Nathaniel has heard enough. He doesn't need this guy's sermons or his pity, so he packs his cart and prepares to leave, the perfect way to let this guy know he's a loudmouthed boor.

"You gave up," says James, the bully of the Ballington. "You push a cart and say, 'I quit. I quit on life.' I can't stand to see you like that. I don't even know you, but I love you as a human being."

It doesn't take a genius to suspect that James is echoing his own experience. But Nathaniel isn't going to indulge his tormentor.

"I didn't quit anything," he tells James.

Pointing to the window of his room, he says:

"That is my place."

20

The thought of loading the Beethoven statue onto a truck in the dead of night and transporting it to room B-116 at the Ballington has occurred to me more than once. Pershing Square is a shabby location for such an iconic figure, and Beethoven is shoved off in a dingy corner of the park. He's been in the square since 1932, when the Philharmonic Orchestra was housed across the street. The sculptor, Arnold Foerster, listened to a string quartet playing Beethoven while he chipped away in his studio. He wanted a disheveled Beethoven lost in thought as he conceived the Ninth Symphony while walking through the woods, hands behind his back holding hat and cane.

It's not as if that statue is the only likeness of Beethoven. Would a bust do the trick? I search the Web and find plenty to choose from, but I can't wait for shipping. I begin checking with local music supply shops, but Adam Crane checks in from the L.A. Philharmonic and tells me to call off the search. They have

Beethoven heads in the Disney Hall gift shop, and he's already picked one out.

Meanwhile, Jennifer's Christmas package for Nathaniel arrives. She has sent clothes and toiletries and photos of their mother, and now I'm ready with my plan. Everyone is in on it. Jennifer, Stuart Robinson, Adam Crane, Peter Snyder. Everyone but Nathaniel, my unsuspecting mark. At his next lesson, his room will no longer be a room but a shrine to his gods. And a home.

"I've got to tell you, I have a good feeling about this," Snyder says when I pick him up at Disney Hall. He's carrying a couple of gifts for Nathaniel, including an L.A. Philharmonic T-shirt.

Nathaniel is already in the room when we arrive, taping things to the wall. He's making it his own, with a map of the United States going up, along with a newspaper story about *The Color Purple* on Broadway. He also has an ad for Baby Magic lotion and is laminating it with half a roll of Scotch tape.

"There's magic in the baby's eyes," he says. "It's Caroline, isn't it?"

Sharing the same wall is a photo of Neil Diamond.

"What's with Neil Diamond?" I ask, wondering if his song "Sweet Caroline" is the association Nathaniel has made.

Nathaniel gives me a quizzical expression and then reexamines the rhinestone cowboy.

"I thought that was you," he says.

Okay. I've got no response to that.

"This is going to be an early Christmas party for you," I tell Nathaniel as I set Jennifer's Christmas gift on his bed.

The first thing he pulls out is a black-and-white photo of a very attractive, smartly dressed woman of about forty who bears a strong resemblance to Nathaniel. He holds the photo at arm's length, quietly reverent.

"That's my mother," he says in a hushed tone, giving her a long look.

He sets the photo on the bed while he goes through the rest of the box, saying the collection of goods is unmistakably Jennifer's doing. She has sent him a package very like one their mother would have sent. Socks, deodorant, a pair of sneakers just the right size.

As he looks through the booty, I take the photo of his mother and stand it on the dresser, asking if that's okay with him.

"That looks good there," Nathaniel says.

Next he opens the small square box I've brought, a gift from Adam Crane. Nathaniel sticks his hand into the Styrofoam packing pellets and pulls out a head.

"Oh, my God!" Nathaniel exclaims. "It's Beethoven!"

I take the bust and set it on the dresser next to Nathaniel's mother.

"What do you think?" I ask.

He approves.

"Beethoven can watch over you in here now," Snyder tells him.

I hand Nathaniel a gift from a reader and he opens it to find a book about the Juilliard school. "I don't want to open it," he says. "I want to imagine what it would be like to be back at my school."

When he gets to the business of the lesson, Nathaniel shows
Snyder what he's accomplished on "Song of the Birds," and he also
shows off the work he's been doing on Schubert's Arpeggione.

"Jesus," Snyder whispers as he watches his student perform.
"The man feels every note."

It was a fairly typical performance by Nathaniel. Some leaps
and crashes, some issues with pitch, some moments of brilliance.
Snyder offers encouragement on the Casals piece and Nathaniel's
smile stretches wide.

"There was no way I was going to ignore that assignment,
because I want to record," Nathaniel says.

Snyder politely tells him there's a lot of work ahead, but it's
smart to set goals and work toward them. He suggests focusing
on "Song of the Birds," and offers to one day accompany him
on piano.

"But can we do a recital?" Nathaniel demands.

"You must keep your dreams," Snyder responds.

They work on rhythm and pitch in a lesson that runs nearly
two hours. This room has meaning to Nathaniel now. He's made
it his and filled it with music, and with his mother and Beethoven
watching over him, I don't know how he'll walk away.

"Our mother would be so proud of all the attention you are
getting because of your talent," Jennifer has written in the card
that lies on the bed next to Nathaniel while he plays his cello. "I
know Momma is smiling from heaven because she is so happy to
know you have a place to lay your head."

Nathaniel plays Bach and Beethoven as if he's a young student
again, the music filled with a sense of urgency and possibility.

Every few minutes he turns toward the dresser, checking in with his mother and his muse.

Will he spend the night?

There's no point in asking or prodding. My case has been made, and after the lesson I walk away, knowing he's in charge. He's always been in charge, this man of the streets, who once said he and his music belonged outdoors, where "the wings of the pigeons sound like the audience clapping."

21

As the year turns over, room B-116 remains a shrine but does not become a home. Nathaniel sleeps in the tunnel, Skid Row is largely unchanged, and I begin to lose faith. In him. In Lamp. In myself. Sure, Nathaniel's situation is better today than it was when I met him nearly a year ago, and my once- or twice-weekly meetings with him still have their rewards. But all the high points, in retrospect, were a tease. I wanted to believe they promised a breakthrough, but such optimism seems delusional now.

Pete Snyder's schedule will allow only one lesson a month or so, and Lamp isn't going to keep a light on for Nathaniel indefinitely. Meanwhile, my teacher is willing to let me try fiddling with his cello, but always finds an excuse not to conduct the lesson in his room. It would probably be wise of me to let go and move on, the way Nathaniel's family has done. But it's almost impossible to escape him. Driving home from work, he's often there in the tunnel, and I find it a relief to know he's okay. I reach to hit my horn, decide not to and drive home, feeling guilty and inept.

Maybe it's that emotion, or a developing savior complex, that has driven me to the Third Street tunnel, where Ernest Adams, a fifty-six-year-old African-American, has taken up residence again after the baseball-bat beating that nearly killed him.

"You wanna feel this?" Adams asks, taking off his ball cap.

Not really. He was beaten like a holiday piñata six months earlier, and the dent in his head is the size of the San Fernando Valley. To be polite, I run a finger over the damage as the hair rises on my neck. It's impossible not to imagine the two young thugs cruising for trouble that night, juiced up on a bum-bashing video. Did they first consider Nathaniel, a block away? If so, was he saved only because he was awake, working out a few kinks in the Elgar Cello Concerto?

Adams was asleep when they came. He has no recollection of their approach, of the bats on his skull, of the bone fragments being driven into his brain. For a man who was on life support at County-USC before his transfer to Rancho Los Amigos for rehab, Adams looks remarkably good. He's smiling like a survivor who can't believe he's made it back from the brink. Brady Westwater, a downtown resident who has known Adams for years, thinks the brain injury has exaggerated a speech impediment, making Adams speak a little slower than before. The beating also blinded Adams in his left eye, which is now milky and blank, and he says doctors told him his sight would never return.

So why has he returned to the very spot where he was left for dead?

Adams, it turns out, is different from Nathaniel in one significant way. Whereas Nathaniel sticks to himself as much as possible, Adams lives for human contact. That's why he has come back, he tells me. He was a familiar face to so many people who took comfort in seeing him, and he can't let them down.

"I was kind of hoping this would be the impetus to get him to make a change and get off the streets," says James Velarde, a friend who lives nearby and visited Adams in the hospital, first at County-USC and later at Rancho Los Amigos.

As I stand out here with Adams and Westwater, the column is already taking shape in my head. This isn't just a nice little feature about the recovery of a man beaten to within an inch of his life. It's an opening for a rant about a screwy system in which Adams was rescued from death only to be sent back to the scene of the crime at his own peril. I call his doctor at Rancho Los Amigos and she tells me arrangements were made for Adams to continue his recovery at a nursing home, but he refused to go. In cases like that, says the doctor, a patient's rights are paramount. He can do as he pleases, whether it's in his best interest or not. The hospital will offer cab fare or bus tokens to a patient who has no other transportation, and he can go wherever he wishes.

"That's the best we can do?" I ask the doctor. Adams is having trouble speaking after a brutal clubbing, and he's been given a free ride straight back into harm's way. At the very least, shouldn't a social worker have been assigned to check and make sure he wasn't crawling around in a gutter or wandering into traffic outside the tunnel?

The doctor doesn't disagree with the thrust of my concern, but she says the law is the law, and the hospital is bound by it. By now I'm tired of hearing about the law. Because of the law, the hospital didn't call Adams's mother to tell her he was being released. He's an adult, so she has no right to know unless he wants her to. Because of the law, friends who hoped to talk Adams into a new and safer life indoors were not informed of his release, despite their humane requests.

"I want to be out here," Adams says, as if this is Beverly Hills. "I want to be my own man, to be under nobody's care. I don't drink, I don't do drugs. I read the Bible, and I want to get the good life the right way."

Maybe he'll leave eventually, he says, but at the moment he's on a mission from God. Unnamed detractors have challenged the very existence of the savior, he claims, and his purpose in life is to show them God has his back, and that the good people outnumber the bad.

"Princes walk upon the face of the earth and hold the reins, while peasants ride on horses," he says.

A man approaches and asks the three of us if anyone can spare a buck. Adams is the first to reach into his pocket.

Westwater and I move out of earshot while Adams talks to the man. We need to get him back to Rancho Los Amigos, says Westwater. He needs a checkup, and maybe the hospital can help him sign up for Social Security disability, which would pay for a place to live.

Lord help me. Here we go again.

"I'm really glad I did this," Adams says on our way back downtown after a visit to Rancho Los Amigos in the town of Downey.

His doctors have just told him his recovery is proceeding nicely, and he's been approved for a Social Security disability check that will cover the cost of housing if he chooses to move indoors. Adams claims, at least, that he's ready to do just that.

It occurs to me, as we cruise the Harbor Freeway past the University of Southern California and the Memorial Coliseum, that I'm doing things I've never done before, and breaking my own standards of journalistic distance and objectivity in the process. Even a columnist, with a license to advocate for one thing or another, generally stops short of personal involvement in the life of a subject. It's important to keep your judgment sharp and your motives pure. But I've been more than an advocate in the cases of Adams and Nathaniel. I've been a social worker for both, and a friend to Nathaniel. Does it have something to do with their personalities and predicaments? No doubt, but it feels as though there's more at play. After thirty years of fulminating about this or that, always from a safe distance and usually to no avail, I want something more, even if it involves the risk of failure. It's not just a journalistic calculation, but a matter of curiosity and a desire for meaning. I envy the doctors who saved Adams's life. I admire the musicians who can hear and appreciate Nathaniel's genius. I'm inspired by the Stuart Robinsons and their patience and grace.

It's Nathaniel who has me thinking this way. I deal too often with people who are programmed, or have an agenda, or guard their feelings. Nathaniel is a man unmasked, his life a public display. We connect in part because there is nothing false about him, and I come away from every encounter more attuned to my own feelings than I would be after, say, an interview with the mayor or the governor. Nathaniel turns my gaze inward. He has me examining what I do for a living and how I relate to the world as a journalist and as a citizen. Despite the many frustrations he presents, I'll never have a richer reward than knowing him well enough to tell his story.

As we reach downtown, I tell Adams I hope Nathaniel will come around just as he has. It's a bit strange that Westwater is still on the phone, trying to find an apartment for a man who doesn't have one, while Nathaniel refuses to move into one that sits empty. Maybe the two of them can room together, I suggest to Adams.

"He's more stubborn than you are," I tell him.

"Oh yes, I've seen him," Adams says. "If he doesn't watch out, he's going to get himself into trouble."

I have no idea what he means.

"He gets into arguments," Adams explains. "He's very confrontational."

I know about the daily disputes in the Lamp courtyard, but Nathaniel leaves there each day for the solitude of the Second Street tunnel. As I think about it, though, I recall seeing Nathaniel do something recently that was out of character. I was driving by and saw him playing violin as a cyclist approached. Nathaniel leaped up and lunged at him as if he intended to knock him off his bike. I couldn't imagine that Nathaniel really intended to do anything other than mark his territory, because I'd heard him complain about cyclists whizzing by perilously close. But the cyclist shook his head angrily.

"What exactly have you seen?" I ask Adams.

"A nasty argument," he says. Also with a cyclist.

The same one, possibly?

Adams says Nathaniel was lugging his cart through the Third Street tunnel in the direction of Skid Row when he got into it with the guy. Adams doesn't know what started the skirmish, but Nathaniel began taunting the guy.

"He had a gun, and he was ready to use it," Adams says of the cyclist.

"He had a gun?"

"He said it took every ounce of strength for him to keep from blowing your friend away."

The minute I drop Adams off, I go looking for Nathaniel. He isn't anywhere near the tunnels. I try Pershing Square, then the Lamp courtyard. I zigzag through Skid Row for an hour. No sign of him. Angry and scared, I drive back to the office and try to distract myself with the backed-up phone calls and e-mails and the business of the next column, whatever it might be. I tell myself he'll be fine because he always is. After work I make the rounds again, driving by the Central Library, too. I park and go inside, hoping to find him foraging for sheet music, but he's nowhere. At Lamp, Robinson is gone and no one else knows anything.

"I'm sure he's fine," Alison tells me at home, although I know she's worried, too. For Nathaniel and for me.

I give it another try around midnight, driving the same route. This time I go back to his old spot at Los Angeles and Winston streets and there's someone sleeping there, but without a shopping cart. That can't be him. Should I call the police, the hospitals or the morgue?

Tuesday morning, January 31, 2006.

Nathaniel's birthday.

The phone rings at 7:30, one of those rings that catches you by surprise and raises your skin. I peek at the caller ID and sit back again. It's a 1-800 telemarketer.

I'm anxious and afraid to call Lamp. Robinson won't be in for a while, so I hold off and read the paper, play with Caroline at her coloring table, pay a few bills. None of this gives me a moment's peace. Finally, I head downtown.

My first stop is the Second Street tunnel, then Pershing Square. I don't know where to go next. I dial Lamp and Robinson takes my call.

He's not anywhere, I tell him, frantically relating Ernest Adams's story about the gun. I tell him I've checked everywhere except with the police and the hospitals, but those will be next.

"Has there been any sign of him over there?" I ask.

"Yeah," Robinson says in a sly, relaxed tone. "He's right here."

Thank you, thank you, thank you.

I don't know what he's been up to, I tell Robinson, but he wasn't in any of his usual spots. I checked the tunnel three times last night.

"Do you have any idea where he was?" I ask.

"Yes," Robinson says. "He spent the night in his apartment."

He what?

I pull the car over to avoid driving up on a curb. Almost exactly one year after our first encounter, he did it.

He did it.

He did it.

Hallelujah!

"Are you kidding?" I ask Robinson.

"No," he says with a giddy laugh.

"I don't believe it," I tell him.

"You want to come see him?"

I want more than that. I want to throw a party, hire a band and make Nathaniel the conductor.

After dinner the night before, Nathaniel had dropped his head, exhausted. It wasn't the spaghetti that had done him in, although that might have helped. He was just exhausted. Thirty-five years of running can do that. Thirty-five years of staying busy to keep from coming unraveled.

"Can I stay in my room tonight?" he asked Robinson when dinner was done.

Robinson had to leave for home and left the matter with one of his staffers, uncertain that Nathaniel would follow through. He didn't know until the next day that his aide opened B-116 and watched Nathaniel pull the cart inside and close the door. That was it. At the prospect of once more hauling all his possessions to the tunnel a mile away, up and down curbs and squeezing through traffic, the fight went out of him.

Casey and Shannon, Patricia and Stuart were right all along. He would do it, but in his own time. It couldn't be forced, it couldn't be rushed and it couldn't be helped by calling the police and having him cuffed and confined. That would have been a disaster. Nathaniel was in charge, and our role was simply to be there, holding a door open for him.

Nathaniel's breakthrough makes me all the more appreciative of what he's been up against. I wonder if the confrontations in the tunnels might have been the expression of his last fight against a move inside. And I think there was something to Robinson's observation that taking the apartment meant having something to lose. It also meant closing the door to just himself and the voices, and perhaps to the frightful recognition of his illness and of the lost years. It was the first step in a return to the world of rules and expectations, a world in which he'd snapped. Moving inside was perhaps riskier and more courageous than walking into a room at Juilliard, at the age of nineteen, for an audition. Here, the stakes were much higher.

I drive straight over to Lamp and find him in the courtyard, drumming his cello case with his fingers.

"Oh, Mr. Lopez," he says, behaving as if nothing has changed.

I hold back an urge to hug him. I don't want to make so big a deal of it that he starts questioning his move. But I can't let this development pass without acknowledging it.

"I looked for you out at the tunnel last night and couldn't find you," I tell him.

"Yeah. I slept in the apartment."

"Oh, you did? How was it?"

"I was worried I wouldn't be able to hear any of the street noises I like. But I heard planes and sirens, and the faucet dripped all night. It was great."

He says he soaked his feet in a bucket and took a hot shower, but the best part of the deal was washing all the bugs out of his clothes.

"Nathaniel, what day did you tell me was your birthday?"

"Oh," he says. "That's January thirty-first."

"Today is your birthday," I tell him. "Did you know today is the thirty-first?"

"It is?"

"Yes. You woke up in your own apartment on your fifty-fifth birthday. Happy birthday, Nathaniel."

Robinson suggests that before I bake a cake and hang streamers in B-116, or whatever else I might be planning, I should stand back and see how things go over the next few days. He's seen people move out as quickly as they moved in, and at the risk of breaking my heart, he tells me Nathaniel could be one such restless soul.

I ask if there's a time when you can rest assured that someone's safe and in the clear.

I can tell Robinson doesn't want to answer the question.

"I don't think he's ready to be in there full-time yet," he says. "He might never leave the streets altogether."

This is not what I want to hear in our moment of glory. I hope that for once, Robinson is wrong. But he's the practical clinician who has seen it all, and I'm still the emotionally invested novice. Robinson informs me that he's obliged to do something Nathaniel might not like. He isn't running a hostel, and he needs Nathaniel to understand that. The room isn't a place to flop occasionally. It's either going to be his home or he won't be allowed to keep it. That's the way it is with other clients, and Nathaniel isn't going to get a free pass because he's got a buddy who writes for the *Los Angeles Times*.

It's more than a fairness issue, Robinson explains. It's part of the recovery philosophy. One aspect of giving Nathaniel back his dignity is to treat him like an adult. So Robinson is going to explain that if he wants to keep the apartment and show respect for the people who have invested time in his welfare, he has to make a commitment. He's going to have to sign a contract that says he'll sleep in the room at least three nights a week, for starters.

Estimating conservatively, I'd guess there have to be about six hundred things Nathaniel might find objectionable about this deal. First and foremost, he's not a deal maker. The beauty of living on the streets is that there are no forms to fill out, and being forced to sign a contract could drive him right back out there. Then, too, there's the complication of keeping a calendar. He doesn't always know whether it's Tuesday or Friday, and now he's going to be expected to have a date book in his head.

But when Robinson lays his proposition on the table, Nathaniel doesn't hesitate.

"Okay," he says, and he picks Monday, Wednesday and Friday nights.

On Tuesday night, he goes to his room, packs up his things and sleeps in the tunnel.

Wednesday night, he eats dinner at Lamp, goes back to his room, turns out the light and goes to sleep.

He's made it through half a week.

On Thursday night, he packs again and sleeps in the tunnel.

So far, so good. Can he do it? Can he complete his third night indoors and honor the contract?

Friday night, no questions asked, he retires after dinner to room B-116.

Home.

Part Three

22

"*Have you noticed* how different he looks?" asks Shannon Murray. "He looks good, doesn't he?"

He looks cleaned up and rested, like a man who had forgotten what either of those things felt like. The edge is gone, too, and there's a softer look in his eyes. Stuart Robinson says he saw Nathaniel observe clients he had previously ignored or argued with, as if he might be recognizing himself in them. He even offered words of support to a couple of them.

A smarter man than I would nod pleasantly, be grateful for small wonders and go find something to do at least twenty or thirty miles from Skid Row. A smarter man would turn things over to the professionals, who, after all, did most of the work anyway and were right all along about what approach would work best for Nathaniel.

But I'm having trouble moving on. Nathaniel, for all his intractable habits, has nothing on me when it comes to compulsive behavior. There's always a better line than the one I just wrote, or a better column idea than the one I've got lined up for tomorrow. And nothing can be left hanging, whether it's a decision on how to redo the front yard or whether a paranoid schizophrenic should be pushed to take advantage of his recent momentum and go immediately into therapy.

Nathaniel helps answer the last dilemma when I visit his apartment and find him frantically cleaning everything with a squirt bottle of Formula 409 cleaner. The blinds, the windowsills, the floor. A chemical mist fills the air, thick enough to peel paint off the walls, and Nathaniel rushes from one task to another like a man chasing a wrapper blowing in the wind. He goes from baseboard to sink to bathroom, squirting and wiping with a rag, and it wouldn't be a surprise to see him follow a stain pattern into the hall, through the courtyard and out in the street to make all of Skid Row spick-and-span. He finally puts down the bottle, flushes the toilet, washes his hands, squirts and wipes the mirror, runs a finger over the blinds and follows with the rag, then flushes the toilet and washes his hands again. The plumbing is good. The room has a glow. I can't breathe because there's a pint of ammonia in my lungs and Nathaniel isn't done yet, but that's okay.

"You've come a long way," I say, telling him Stuart Robinson is very impressed by the way he seems to be looking after the newer clients. "Maybe you can help some of the people who just came through the door. Anything's possible now, especially if you take advantage of some of the services they've got here for you. The mental health advocates, the people who can help get you signed up on SSI to pay the rent here. The psychiatrists."

"I would support any psychiatrist who will support me," he says without interrupting his fanatical cleanup.

Is it the 409? Has it cut off the oxygen and impaired his thinking? I'm tempted to run through the streets in search of Dr. Prchal and get it going here and now. Yes, Nathaniel goes on, he wants to make his own "contribution to the psychiatric environment." I don't know exactly what that means but it sounds like progress. I ask again if he's serious about seeing a psychiatrist and this time he deflects, saying he might consider it at some point. But as for his own contribution, he'd like to use what he knows to help people.

"I'd want to be a music therapist," he says as he disinfects the bathroom mirror.

Eager to move ahead, I check in with Mark Ragins, my on-call doctor, for some advice on accelerating Nathaniel's transformation. I still refer frequently to Ragins's book *A Road to Recovery* as if it's an owner's manual, and it seems to me that in the doctor's four-stage model, Nathaniel has just moved from No. 2, Empowerment ("Sometimes they need another person to believe in them before they're confident enough to believe in themselves") to No. 3, Self-Responsibility ("Old patterns of dependency must be broken, and mental health professionals need to encourage clients to take charge instead of settling for the ease and safety of being taken care of").

Ragins is glad to hear the news of Nathaniel's breakthrough, but I can hear him chuckling over my sense of urgency. His prescription, more or less, is that rather than rush Nathaniel to the nearest shrink, I get a tranquilizer gun, point it at my hip and pull the trigger.

"I wouldn't push him into therapy right away," he says.

Coming inside was obviously a good sign, but that shouldn't be misread as an indication that the next steps will be any easier than the last, the doctor warns me. Nathaniel will have enough of a challenge adapting to new routines and people, and a lot of that will be scary for him. This is no time, Ragins adds, to remind him of his history with doctors and meds, clinics and hospitals.

What to do, then?

Let him find his way. Be patient. Be his friend.

"Relationship is primary," Ragins says. "It is possible to cause seemingly biochemical changes through human emotional involvement. You literally have changed his chemistry by being his friend."

I don't know if I've ever been a very good friend to anyone, maybe because friendship is too much about the past. Do you know what ever happened to what was his name? Do you remember the time? I'm too busy moving from one city and one job to another, loyal to the rhythms of a column-writing schedule that serves as my metronome. Who has time to look back? Friendship is easier when it has no history, no time for broken promises and all the little piques that fill a running tally sheet. To Nathaniel, as well, the past is irrelevant. Life is all about the next phrase, about feeding the monster, about finding a definition of himself that makes sense for at least one day. We're like each other in many respects. Do you think about writers the way I think about musicians? he asked when I spent that night with him. Yes, I do. But I don't have time to do enough of it.

I don't know if I've truly changed Nathaniel's chemistry, as Ragins suggested. But, yes, of course we're friends by most definitions of the word. I wouldn't consider talking to him about a career move, the way I would with longtime pals, or about the challenges of being a good father and husband while devoting so much time to work. Come to think of it, Nathaniel and I don't really have conversations. Mostly he talks or plays music and I listen. He can't relate to my world and I have trouble relating to his, except for my growing interest in classical music. I can't tell him about having been the victim of identity theft, because I'd have to explain debit cards, and it's all about money, anyway, which holds no interest for him. He looks at me as if I'm an alien when I say I got an e-mail from his sister, Jennifer, and like I'm pretending when I explain that an e-mail is sort of a letter, sent electronically, through cyberspace.

And yet for all that, he's changed my chemistry, too. I've never volunteered for anything, never was a Big Brother or Scout leader, but Nathaniel still has me clearing space in a busy schedule to make time for him. I drive through L.A. enveloped by orchestral music, and I look forward to sharing my new appreciation of it with Caroline, who until now had only one parent with an ear for classical. If a friend is someone who inspires, who challenges, who sends you in search of some truer sense of yourself, Nathaniel is indeed a friend. In my euphoria over his move indoors, he has me thinking I might like to do something other than work for a newspaper. Something in the public service realm and very hands-on, like the Stuart Robinsons and Mary Scullions of the world. But I don't quite know what it would be, or what I'm even qualified to do.

As I leave his apartment one day shortly after he moved in, he calls me back and holds out his hand. It's a long, firm handshake, followed by a smile. I look into his eyes and see the man he's always been behind the racing, spinning madness. The son who lost a father. The musician who lost a chance. No, we don't have too many so-called normal conversations. But what's normal? I hold his hand in mine, and neither of us needs to say a thing.

Darrell Steinberg calls me from Sacramento, where he's putting together a staff to run the business of Prop. 63. Among other things, he needs a communications director.

"Do you know of anyone?" he asks.

I pause. Should I ask him if he'd consider me?

The thought is still scary. But I tell Steinberg I've been wondering if it's time for me to take a risk and start a second career.

"We should at least get together and talk about it," Steinberg says, encouraging me to take the leap.

I tell him I'll get back to him.

Forget it, Alison says. She's not moving to Sacramento. "Maria Shriver doesn't even live there." And I'd be miserable working as a state bureaucrat, she insists.

Maybe so. But *Times* editor Dean Baquet, who replaced John

Carroll, is headed for his own showdown with corporate bosses and could soon be gone as well. After a thrilling run of thirty years, did I want to spend the rest of my career with a scowl, reminiscing about the good old days? I'd been lucky beyond all my expectations, landing one great job after another. I caught brief glimpses of world history in the making (high tea with vanquished Iraqi soldiers in the first Gulf War, ninety-proof vodka with Muscovites celebrating the fall of Communism, diving for cover in a Bosnian graveyard as a funeral procession came under attack) and I chased news across the United States (the eruption of Mount St. Helens in Washington state, the parade of presidential candidates through Iowa and New Hampshire, the trials of assassins and thieves ranging from a New York mobster to a Louisiana governor). I had the privilege of rattling cages and knocking on doors in Philadelphia and Los Angeles, of exposing fools and heralding saints. If I walked away now, no one could say I got cheated.

Just for the heck of it I Google "real estate" and "Sacramento." Dozens of Web sites pop up. I pick one at random and begin clicking on photos of houses all over the area. Sacramento is an hour from where I grew up, so I know the terrain. I like the area just north of there in the Sierra foothills, so I begin looking at houses in Auburn, a gold-rush town with a rustic, old-fashioned downtown. I find a three-bedroom ranch house that backs up to a creek, and the price is roughly half of what my house in Los Angeles is worth.

"Take a look at this," I tell Alison.

"What is it?" she asks.

"It's a house in Auburn. Look at the price."

She pulls back and stands over me. By her posture alone, I know I'm in trouble.

"You're not still thinking about this, are you?"

"Why not? At that price, we could make this work, even if I make half the salary. What do you think of the house?"

She looks again, closer this time.

"I hate it," she says. "And I'm not moving."

"There are lots of others," I tell her.

"You'd go crazy the first day," she fires back. "The highlight of your day is going to be getting up from your desk to go to a meeting. What is the matter with you?"

I don't see the job that way, I tell her. I'd craft it so that I tour the state, talking up good stories to reporters. I'd be able to stay in touch with Nathaniel that way, too, visiting him on swings down to Southern California.

"*You're* a reporter," she points out. "When you know about good stories, guess what? You can write them yourself. You have the perfect job. What's the problem?"

Good point. And she has more.

I've never had a nine-to-five schedule in my life, and one of the things I enjoy about my job is the variety of subjects. I'm a newspaper columnist, she says. That's what I am and who I am, and if I have any sense, I'll try to hang on to the job as long as I can.

23

Two months go by and Nathaniel has been in his room every night without fail. He's up at seven to go to breakfast at Lamp, then back in at seven in the evening. By day he often goes back to the Second Street tunnel to play, and one day a man approaches in the middle of a practice session and sets down a case. Inside is a new cello. "I thought you could use this," says the man, who walks away without giving his name or saying another word. Nathaniel now has two cellos and six violins.

At the Ballington, a monitor lets Nathaniel into his room every night and makes sure he gets up in time for breakfast, but Stuart Robinson is thinking of rewarding Nathaniel for his continued progress by giving him his own key. Nathaniel sits in the dark at night, playing violin or cello for a while and then setting the instruments down and practicing his fingering by tapping lightly on his forearms. He sometimes does this, lying on his back, and keeps at it until he falls asleep in the middle of something beautiful, perhaps the Bach Prelude No. 1 or one of his old stand-bys, the Bloch Prayer or the Schubert Arpeggione.

It feels strange that more than a year into our friendship, Nathaniel hasn't been to my house, which is just five miles from Skid Row. He tells me he'd love to visit, but can't very well fit his cart into my car or push it that far. I tell him he can lock it in his apartment and it'll be fine.

"Oh, no, Mr. Lopez. I can't do that."

"Sure you can."

"Everything will be gone when I return. They'll come through the windows, the vents, under the door. God himself does not know how they get in, but they do."

After several conversations that go no further, I tell Nathaniel I'll look into renting a van big enough to haul his shopping cart. He thinks this is a fine solution, but when I mention it to Casey Horan, she doesn't like the idea.

"We need to get him to let go of that cart," she says. He needs to trust that his apartment is safe, and that he can manage without his rolling security blanket.

The cart really is about security, and letting go of it would be like letting go of the side of the pool for the first time. But there's a method to the man's madness, one that blurs the line once more between insanity and insight. As long as he has the cart, Nathaniel can't very well be expected to visit, say, a psychiatrist. A cart probably wouldn't fit through the door of a doctor's office. And with a buggy in tow, he can't very well be expected to make a complete return to so-called normal life. Like the terrifying life in which he lost his mind while under tremendous pressure at Juilliard. But part of the paradox of my relationship with Nathaniel is that I'm always trying, often in vain, to outsmart him. This time I'm thinking I might be able to do it by appealing to both his sense of tradition and his appetite.

"What'd you eat for breakfast today?" I ask in the Lamp courtyard.

"Oatmeal."

"Was it any good?"

"It was all right. The food here is really not very good, and they poison it with beer and wine."

"I had bacon and eggs. There's nothing like the smell of bacon filling the house in the morning."

"Yeah," he says. "I like bacon and eggs."

"You should come over to the house. How about Easter brunch? We're going to have bacon and eggs, home fries, toast. I promise not to poison the food. Little Caroline will have an Easter egg hunt and we'll fix her a basket with some chocolates. You remember Easter egg hunts when you were a kid? You like chocolate?"

"Yeah, I like chocolate."

"What the heck, then? Would you like to come over? I'll pick you up at your apartment, take you to my place and have you back in no time."

But I can't tie his buggy to my Honda Accord and tow it to my house, I tell him. He'll have to lock it in the apartment, but only for a couple of hours.

Nathaniel asks me to repeat the date. He pulls a scrap of paper out of his shopping cart and writes it down.

"Sunday, April sixteenth. Easter—Mr. Lopez's house. Caroline Lopez. Jeffrey and Andrew Lopez. Mrs. Lopez. Steve Lopez, staff writer."

· · ·

Sunday morning and the house smells of coffee and bacon. My wife and I have prepared a feast and now Caroline wants me to hurry up already and go pick up our guest.

"Where's Mathaniel?" she asks.

Close enough.

I drive downtown, past hordes of people awaking from a night on the pavement. I turn onto East San Julian Street and there he is, waiting at the door of Lamp like a racehorse in the gates. He's wearing a flowery red Hawaiian shirt and a bandanna fashioned from yellow police crime scene tape. He has his cello and violin.

No shopping cart.

"I've been working on Saint-Saëns for Caroline," he says as we load his things into the car. He wants his instruments in the back-seat, not the trunk. To him, that would be like putting children in the trunk.

He apologizes for his appearance as I drive, saying he has done the best he could to spiff himself up. His kinky black hair is wet and trained into place, parted in the middle. He seems okay. No sign of panic. In fact, he is clearly excited about this field trip. I make a point of driving past his old spot at Los Angeles and Winston and then through the Second Street tunnel. I want him to have a reminder of how far he's come. He notes the handful of tunnel dwellers but keeps his thoughts to himself. On Glendale Boulevard, the gray monotony of downtown disappears behind us and the San Gabriel Mountains climb into the clouds up ahead.

"Is this Hollywood?" he asks.

"This is Echo Park. Hollywood's a few miles to the west."

"Los Angeles is a water town, like Cleveland. Lake Erie, Pacific Ocean. But I don't know where it is. Yeah, I've seen it, but I don't know what that means, that this is supposed to be a place on the ocean, Los Angeles, Las Vegas, the Rams of Los Angeles, loss of six yards on the play, when you can't see the water from anywhere. I can't believe how beautiful this is. Do you live in Hollywood, Mr. Lopez? No, you live in Silver Lake. Is that right? Silver Lake?"

Of course, anything would look good after Skid Row, where there is no green, no horizon, nothing but that daily fracas and the inescapable stench of aimless despair. If not for that cart, he might have gotten out more often, out here where the change of scenery can't help but be good for his spirit. In an ideal situation, I'd have a little bit of land and maybe an in-law cottage he could live in and use as a music studio. Of course, in a really ideal situation he wouldn't need me to make it happen for him. He'd decide he wants out of Skid Row, that he's ready to do whatever it takes. Go into treatment. Give meds another shot. Shove that damn cart into the Los Angeles River.

If he sticks with the lessons from Mr. Snyder and gets in more practice time now that he's living indoors, it doesn't seem out of the question that he might one day work with students just like he did with me that day. Maybe he can help the kids over at the Union Rescue Mission, a block from Lamp. About a hundred children live there and I know the director, Andy Bales. He's got a chapel with a stage and a piano, and I'm sure I could work something out with him. A music therapist. That's what Nathaniel says he wants to be. I know it's a long shot, but I don't see why I shouldn't encourage him to work toward that goal.

It takes fifteen minutes to get to my house. Caroline greets Nathaniel at the door with a bashful smile and a half-step of retreat.

"Do you know who this is?" I ask Caroline.

"Mathaniel," she says shyly, a bit overwhelmed by the ensemble, but very much impressed with the yellow bandanna.

"Are you going to play your violin?" she asks as he carefully sets his instruments on the dark wood of the living room floor.

There's no bashfulness on Nathaniel's part. He quickly makes himself at home, acting like an eccentric and gabby uncle who's dropped by after a long absence. He doesn't show quite as much interest in Caroline as I expected, but as an obnoxiously proud dad, I feel that way about everybody. In Nathaniel's case, though, I suppose I'm beginning to think of him as extended family. Having him here seems natural and overdue. He sets up his music stand, his sheet music and a weighted contraption he uses to keep the pin of his cello from sliding on the floor. He sees Alison's piano in the corner of the room, bolts over and bangs out a little jazz riff.

"I didn't know you ever played much piano," I say.

"Oh, I don't play piano, really. That was a little thing I worked out one day at Juilliard and it knocked them out. I don't even know what it was. Did you like it? Really? I just jumped right in and gave it that little vamp. Whoooa! They liked it at Juilliard, or they said they did, anyway. They seemed to like it. Of course, I wasn't a piano man at Juilliard, where you had some of the really talented youngsters from all over the world. Unbelievably talented young maestros from China, Japan, Europe, of course. I don't even know where. A lot of the Yo-Yo Ma type people. Now there was a youngster who was off the charts with talent, like a bird type of performer, out of LaGuardia, JFK, the New York City airports at that time, big birds flying in and out from all over the world, Canada, United States of America."

I'm so accustomed to this kind of rambling that I barely notice the jumble. There's often a thread in there somewhere, it seems to me, or at least a semi-logical association. But when I catch Alison's eye, I know what she's thinking. In Nathaniel's high-anxiety monologue, she hears her brother's voice—the brother she thinks might be bipolar, though he's never been diagnosed as such. She remembers the years of anguish following the change that occurred in his teens, his behavior alternately manic and sullen. I know Alison loves me for loving Nathaniel, and through me she cares about him, too. But I see in her eyes on Easter Sunday that she is afraid of what I'm in for—what all of us are in for. Don't worry, I want to tell her. He's doing fine and he's getting better. Trust me.

Nathaniel flutters about our living room and kitchen, yammering as he sets up to play. Caroline, who is used to holding court and being the only one in the house privileged to talk non-stop, looks like a child who fears she might not get the first piece of cake at her own party. When Nathaniel begins playing Saint-Saëns, Caroline stops and stares at him and his cello. She saw him play once before, near the tunnel, but now the music is in her house and she can hear it and feel it coming up through the floor-boards. She's mesmerized, at least for a minute, and I envy Nathaniel's ability all the more. His music has warmed the house and captured my daughter's attention.

Nathaniel stays on his high through breakfast and gratefully examines the goodies in the Easter basket we fixed for him (chocolate treats, nuts, socks and toothpaste). He unexpectedly throws out a few words in French and before I can ask what he's saying he sings a line of Italian opera. I tell Alison she should hear his Shakespearean delivery. Nathaniel happily obliges, and it's as if the Prince of Denmark has joined us for breakfast, punctuating his soliloquy with a fork. "To die, to sleep, To sleep—perchance to dream—ay, there's the rub, for in that sleep of death what dreams may come, when we have shuffled off this mortal coil, must give us pause."

The transformation of this man who jumped back in fear at our first meeting is dizzying. At the moment he's entirely unguarded and free, reveling in his own resurrection. He seems to be savoring the day, the food, the company. "Look at this child," he says, taking in Caroline as if her existence is an act of divinity. "I can't believe that you can create a little person like that. I'd like to start a family, too. I don't know if that's even possible."

He's looking at me, waiting for a response. I look across the table at Alison, whose expression tells me I'm on my own. I don't really know what to say. It's heartbreaking to hear him express what he's missed in life, and just as tragic for him to trust that it might still be within reach.

"Of course it is," I say. "You're only two years older than I am. But you're busy enough with other things for now, don't you think?"

We head out back after our meal. I want him to feel a fresh

breeze blow in from the lake and across the redwood deck that sits on top of my garage, with a view of eighty-year-old houses hugging the canyon, the Griffith Observatory and the Hollywood sign in the western distance. It's hard not to feel a touch of guilt. Look at what I have here in this enclave of million-dollar homes, five miles from the squalor and hard limits of Skid Row. Look at my wife, and my daughter, and my health. But for all his longing about a family of his own, and despite what might have been, Nathaniel seems free of self-pity for now.

"Words do not express thoughts very well," he says, quoting Hermann Hesse as he readies for a concert under sunny skies while Caroline spins circles around him on her tricycle. I call Jennifer in Atlanta and hand him the phone.

"Happy Easter to you, too," Nathaniel says giddily, telling his sister he can see the Hollywood sign across the hills and canyons. He is radiant, and happier than I've ever seen him. A neighbor looks down curiously from a nearby balcony at my guest with the yellow crime scene bandanna. Nathaniel says to his sister: "I'm with Mr. Lopez and Mrs. Lopez and little Caroline. I can see the Hollywood sign, Jennifer. I never knew Los Angeles could be so beautiful."

Adam Crane of the Los Angeles Philharmonic is thrilled at the news of Nathaniel's move indoors and other signs of progress, and he makes a standing offer for him to attend concerts at Disney Hall. Is Nathaniel up for it? I wonder. He's a different man than the one who attended the rehearsal six months earlier. Either that, or I'm simply more comfortable around him. I do know that any mention of Disney Hall launches him into a reverie, and it happens again when I ask if he'd like to see a chamber music performance.

"I would like that very much," he says.

"You understand it would be a concert this time, not a rehearsal?"

No problem, he says. The concerns he had six months ago, about being in a crowd and feeling out of place, are gone. His only issue, he tells me, is the program, explaining that Serenade in D major, Op. 8, Piano Trio No. 3 in C minor, Op. 1, No. 3, and String

Quartet No. 5 in A major, Op. 18, No. 5, are not among Beethoven's more celebrated works, nor will we see the entire orchestra "in its full complement."

Don't worry, I tell him. We have a standing invitation to attend concerts, and this may well be the first of many.

Once again, Crane greets us in the lobby and gives Nathaniel VIP treatment, escorting us to our seats and waging another lively discussion about the program. Nathaniel's clothes are neater and cleaner this time, his grooming more meticulous. He sits quietly for two hours, perfectly at ease, with an occasional rhythm tap on his leg or a "bravo."

Less than a month later, we return to see the Philharmonic perform Beethoven's Fifth and Eighth Symphonies. Nathaniel calls me a few days before the concert to ask if he can bring along a woman named Pam, whom he met while she was working on a documentary about Skid Row musicians. Sure, I tell him, although I'm not sure what his interest in her might be. She's just a friend, he says. I take Alison, too, and the four of us have a lovely Sunday afternoon at Disney Hall. Crane escorts us to the same section where we sat the last time, and Nathaniel is in a particularly good mood. I'm wondering if it's because Pam is here. She's a bright and attractive woman several years younger than Nathaniel, and I feel just the slightest tug of concern. I remember his comment at my house about wanting to start his own family, and wonder if he has feelings for Pam that will only hurt him in the end.

Crane excuses himself just before the program begins, telling us he's filling in as the announcer for the day. Nathaniel spots Peter Snyder and Ben Hong onstage and says each of their names quietly, smiling happily. Then we hear Crane's voice, and Nathaniel says his name, too. The last thing Crane says over the PA system is that the concert is being recorded, and he asks that all applause be held until the room returns to quiet after each piece. More than two thousand people hear this request, and only one will ignore it. At the end of the Eighth Symphony, a single patron has been stirred to a level of uncontrollable passion. He scoots up in his seat as the last note is struck, and before the sound subsides completely, he unleashes a lone "Bravo!"

Nathaniel.

If Nathaniel's mind plays tricks on him, so, too, does mine. I make myself believe anything is possible. Moments like those at Easter and at Disney Hall reveal a man who is charming, witty and full of passion. The growth on the upside of his potential is so great, I deceive myself into thinking that his darker moments will diminish as he continues to get better. I suppose there's a degree of selfishness involved. Not only do I genuinely want him to get better but I want to be able to say that I helped make it happen. Yes, there's ego involved, as much as I'd like to believe otherwise, and my sacrifices would make more sense if a happy ending were taking shape. So when people ask me how Nathaniel is doing, I don't tell them that he's still writing on the walls of his apartment, occasionally scratching out a swastika or saying that smokers should be put to death. I don't tell them that on some days he sprinkles talcum powder on his face and calls himself Mr. White, or that he occasionally uses a brassiere as a scarf and has no explanation as to why, nor any acknowledgment as to how odd it appears. My motive, in part, is to protect him and to defend his dignity. When people ask how he's doing, I'm more inclined to tell them that Disney Hall patrons were straining during intermission to hear the erudite observations of my sophisticated friend Nathaniel, who has a way to go but is coming along nicely. Maybe another of my deceptions is thinking I have the constitution and patience to work in the mental health field full-time. Alison was right about me in that regard, and though I haven't given up entirely on the idea of a career change, and have even talked to the head of a nonprofit organization about a possible job, I've decided to stick with the column for now.

One day in the Lamp courtyard, a client puts my limitations as an amateur social worker in perspective when he offers both a reality check and a critique.

"When are you going to write the real story about your friend Nathaniel?" he asks.

"What do you mean?"

"I mean the way he treats people around here."

"And what do you mean by that?"

"The names he has for people. He's got a mouth on him. If you're not black you're a white bitch. That kind of thing."

I've learned it's not uncommon for people with schizophrenia to be hyperreligious or hyper–race-conscious. But I didn't realize Nathaniel had descended into daily confrontations with fellow clients at Lamp.

"We do have some issues," Stuart Robinson says when I ask what's going on.

It usually begins with someone violating the supreme command-

ments in Nathaniel's nonnegotiable code of human conduct—
thou shalt not smoke cigarettes, and thou shalt not flick the butts.
In his mind, the guilty deserve nothing less than an eternity in
hell, roasting in fields of smoldering ash. The man of the arts who
was so eloquent at my house and in the company of world-class
musicians calls the offenders niggers, white bitches and fags, and
if they don't like it he stands his ground with clenched fists, ready
to back up his convictions.

Is it possible that I barely know Nathaniel, that my perspective is blurred by both my own selfish desires and the fact that he
is usually on his best behavior in my presence? The more I visit,
the more I catch glimpses of this darker Nathaniel.

"That's the kind of niggerly behavior that gives all of us a bad
name," he tells me one day when two black clients, both of them
smoking, have a belligerent argument about which one owes the
other a dollar. Nathaniel's rage rises as theirs does, as if he's feeding on it. "Yeah, get another dollar and go buy some more cigarettes and take those drugs that are *killing* the women and children
of Los Angeles. White plague, bubonic plague, sickle-cell anemia.
You're killing yourselves *and you're killing me!*"

I try to calm him but he says this has got to stop. These people
shouldn't be allowed in here and something's got to be done
about it. I tell him I'll talk to Stuart Robinson and he tells me I
better tell someone else, too, because Stuart Robinson "isn't man
enough to do his job."

He's just having a bad day, I tell myself, though I know it's
more than that. The man who came to my house exists in full,
and I suspect he'll resurface. But this Nathaniel is as real as the

other, and he now seems to be spending as much time courting trouble as he used to spend playing cello and violin. This is what Mollie Lowery was talking about when she warned me that recovery is not linear. Sometimes it's a step forward, sometimes it's a step back, and sometimes you can't tell the difference. Solutions create new problems. Nathaniel has become part of a community, but it puts him into daily conflict with others. He's got an apartment, but he has begun upsetting neighbors and management by drawing on the walls inside and out.

What do I do now?

Six months after the mayor of Los Angeles put Skid Row on his fix-it list, the Midnight Mission plays host to a busload of public officials, including President Bush's homeless czar, celebrating the release of a ten-year plan to end homelessness in Los Angeles County. The plan doesn't look bad on paper, as far as it goes, although any government plan that aims to end any monumental social problem is doomed to fail. To end homelessness, the county supervisors would have to end poverty, fix the schools, build several dozen Lamps, provide health insurance to those without, solve the affordable-housing crisis and develop a living-wage economy, none of which is in this plan. The key feature of the $100 million proposal is a call for five regional centers to handle the county's estimated ninety thousand homeless, but even that is a long shot, because there isn't a single community that wants to host anything resembling Skid Row. Philip Mangano,

President Bush's point man, takes the microphone to proclaim that the suffering of so many people is a disgrace, and L.A. county supervisor Zev Yaroslavsky agrees that the time is right for change. "We've got some momentum politically to do something about this, we've got some money to attach to that political momentum, and it may be an opportunity that will not pass our way again in our political lifetimes."

I'm listening, but I'm not entirely in the room. This meeting has brought out a caravan of TV news trucks in part because of the Skid Row coverage by my colleagues and Nathaniel's story, but he's already getting the kind of help the public officials are talking about, and I'm not sure how much good it will do him in the long run. It took me a year to lure him inside, and now he's in the Lamp courtyard a half block from this meeting place, creating yet another disturbance for all I know. As the meeting proceeds, I get handshakes and whispered notes of gratitude from Skid Row providers who thank me for helping bring attention to their plight. I feel awkward and unworthy, and out of the corner of my eye I see someone else approach. But this guy has no intention of congratulating me.

It's a downtown resident I've seen before, and I've heard that he is among the critics who think my only interest in Skid Row is personal glory.

"How much?" he keeps asking.

Several heads turn and I feel the blood fill my face. I'm half embarrassed and half enraged.

How much money am I making for exploiting Skid Row? he continues. How much for exploiting Nathaniel? He hears I'm writing a book about it all. How much will I give Nathaniel?

My pulse quickens and my ears burn. All I can hear is "How much? How much? How much?"

I ignore him until I no longer can, finally leaning down to this shaggy-haired man, who is a head shorter than I.

"It's none of your business," I tell him.

He keeps at it, and I know I should ignore him or leave. But I feel, insanely, as if I have to respond, so I lead him into the hallway. We're followed by a Midnight Mission employee and two senior officers who are at the meeting with the county sheriff. They've seen something in my eyes that worries them.

Through gritted teeth, I tell my tormentor that my book and my relationship with Nathaniel are none of his business, and I don't appreciate his putting on a sideshow at a public meeting. But saying this doesn't begin to calm me; it only pushes me further out of control. A voice in my head tells me to back off, but I can't. Is this how a person feels before a coronary? I'm trembling now, my jowls quivering as I tap his shoulder with a finger. All that stops me from losing it and doing something really stupid is the thought of what a story it would make if I'm hauled away a twitching mess, perhaps in a straitjacket, from a meeting about the horrors of Skid Row.

"This is none of your business!" I tell him one last time, as if it will mean anything. He's already gotten the best of me. I withdraw and return to the meeting out of breath. At the first sign that it's about to break up, I head for the exit.

Everything I've written about Nathaniel is extremely personal, and yet I've shared it with thousands of readers. Have I exploited him? Is it possible for me to keep writing about him without doing so? I've asked myself the question before, and the answer remains the same. I'm telling the story of his courage, his challenge and his humanity, and I believe there's a benefit to him, to me and to the public. If I'm overly sensitive to criticism, it's because I'm frustrated by my own limitations, and because I don't know whether, in the end, I'll have had as big an impact on Nathaniel's life as he will have had on mine.

25

The one thing I do know is that I can't sit by, waiting for Nathaniel to self-destruct. The solution is so obvious I can't believe I didn't think of it sooner. A music studio. If he has a place to go, other than Lamp, and other than his apartment, it would get him out of the fray, give him some privacy and a purpose. It would almost be like going to work each day, or to school. He could wake up, have breakfast and head over to his studio to practice or take lessons. I'm not thinking of anything fancy, and not a recording studio, per se. Any old storefront might do. If he feels like it, he can put up a thousand "No Smoking" signs, hang the Marlboro man in effigy, whatever. Ideally, it would be nice to set him up several miles from Skid Row, but how would I get him there each day? For better or worse, Nathaniel considers this his neighborhood. So I begin cruising the area in search of "For Rent" signs, thinking I might be able to cover the cost before gentrification drives everything up and out of sight. But I find that, even on Skid Row, the prices are way out of my range.

Casey Horan has a solution.

The other Lamp facility, two blocks from where Nathaniel lives, is about to be remodeled. Horan says she can figure a music studio into the plans, and although it wouldn't be exclusively for Nathaniel, he can use it pretty much as he pleases.

"We could give him the title of artist in residence," Horan says.

It's brilliant.

"A *studio?* I have a studio."

"You have a studio apartment. This would be a music studio."

"You mean like Disney Hall?"

"Not quite that fancy."

"A recording studio, with Sony or something like that, where we could make recordings? Could you call someone at Sony?"

"This might be a little more modest than that, but I guess you could make recordings in there if you wanted to. You could practice with Mr. Snyder, and you could teach all the people here who want to learn music. You could give me lessons again, if you don't think that would drive both of us crazy."

He's intrigued but says if there's going to be a studio, it should be up at Disney Hall.

"I don't want to have to deal with all the hooligans and thieves who would steal everything and treat the studio like an ashtray," he says. "These are people who don't give a hoot about anything but their drug habits and their nonsense, and I'm not puttin' up with any of that ridiculous behavior from those knuckleheads. They cannot be trusted in Los Angeles, they cannot be trusted in New York City, they cannot be trusted in Cleveland, Ohio, polluting themselves and destroying their minds with the drug known as tobacco."

"You'd be artist in residence," I argue. "We're going to have to come up with a name for it."

"A name for what?"

"Your new studio."

"I don't want any studio. I don't need any studio. I already have my apartment."

"That's not big enough for you to play music with friends. I haven't told you yet, but someone has a piano they want to donate to you."

"A piano?"

"One of my readers. She read a column about you and said she has a piano she doesn't use anymore. We can put it in the new studio. You can play it yourself or have someone accompany you while you're on cello or violin. I'd love to hear you on bass, too, if we could ever find you a string bass."

"I can put the piano in my apartment."

"It won't fit."

"Is it a grand, or a baby grand?"

"No, I think it's an upright, but you barely have room to sleep in your apartment. We need to put the piano in your new studio so you can jam in there with other musicians. Now, what do you want to call the studio?"

He insists that if it really happens, he wants the studio to be used for art shows, poetry readings and theater productions in addition to music.

"That's up to you," I tell him. "You're going to be the artist in residence. Maybe you can do *Hamlet* and take the lead."

He has a suggestion for a name.

"The Beethoven, Mr. Lopez, Little Walt Disney Concert Hall and Performing Arts Theater of Los Angeles, California."

Too long, I tell him. And it should say something about Cleveland or the Settlement School, where he studied under Harry Barnoff.

"I've got it," he says. "The Lopez Beethoven Settlement West Studio of Los Angeles, Home of Beethoven."

Whatever it will be called, the studio won't be a reality for weeks, if not months, and in the meantime Nathaniel is dismissing my every suggestion that he follow up on his promise to consider seeing a doctor. I remind him that his very words were "I would support any psychiatrist who will support me." But now he insists he doesn't need help, and says no member of the medical profession can be trusted. I tell him I've met lots of people with schizophrenia who get up in the morning and go to work or school, raise families and live productive lives with the help of regular care and medication. Nathaniel tells me that in Cleveland he was arrested and taken to mental hospitals too many times to count, and he's ingested every psychotropic drug known to man. Nobody, he says, is going to do that to him again.

"There's a new generation of drugs," I tell him. "People who had problems with the old drugs say the new ones work better and have fewer side effects."

"Yeah, well, I don't need any of that."

. . .

My mother and father called me a hardhead in Italian and Spanish when I was a boy, and Alison settles for English. In any language, it's true. I must have inherited some of the immigrant pluck my parents grew up with as first-generation Californians, or in my case, maybe it's just plain stubbornness. I suspect this has something to do with my continued scheming to get Nathaniel together with Dr. Prchal. Though she has met him, I don't think he knows she's a psychiatrist. So what if she just happens to be with me one day when I stop in to see Nathaniel, and the three of us chat about this and that? She'll be an acquaintance, not a doctor. With a few visits like that, she might be able to seduce him into treatment, as she herself suggested that night at Little Pedro's Blue Bongo.

"Okay," Prchal says. "Let's give it a try."

She agrees to meet Nathaniel and me before work one day, at 7 A.M., in the Lamp courtyard. Nathaniel and I arrive within seconds of each other, and I know the moment I see him that we're in for trouble. Nathaniel is tight, his face full of shadows. When Prchal arrives he barely acknowledges her. Prchal and I sit at one of the picnic tables and Nathaniel stands over us, keeping his distance and looking as though he's deciding whether to bolt.

"Nathaniel, I brought Ms. Prchal here today because I know you've had some issues with the management. Casey Horan was out of town so I thought maybe you'd like to talk to Ms. Prchal about what's been troubling you."

Prchal's face is drawn, her mouth tight. I wonder if I've just blown it by suggesting she's an administrator. She, in turn, introduces herself as a doctor, and Nathaniel shoots me a look. Uh-huh, he seems to be thinking. You set me up.

I have such a bad feeling about where this is headed, I consider calling the whole thing off. But it's already too late.

"The problem I have is that the so-called staff of this place is horrible," Nathaniel says, shaking his fist in the direction of Stuart Robinson's second-floor office. "The issue I have is that nobody here knows how to do their goddamn job because they are imbeciles, and they are a DISGRACE, and I will not have any of these motherFUCKERS tell me what I can or cannot do, when they do not have one ounce of ability to do their own motherfucking jobs because they are inept, ignorant, horrible bastards who cannot perform the simplest aspect of their sworn duties."

His eyes are red with rage. I've never seen this side of him and I have no idea what might come next. I discreetly position my feet so that if he leaps at Prchal, I can try to protect her. I don't really expect him to do such a thing, but I can't read him and I can't be sure. Something unrecognizable burns in his eyes. I try to stay perfectly calm, speaking to him in a normal tone in the hope of bringing down the temperature a degree or two. Mr. Robinson, I tell him, has a lot of responsibility and handles it to the best of his ability. But this only makes it worse.

"Mr. Robinson does not DO his job. Mr. Robinson does not know HOW to do his job, because if he KNEW how to do it, I wouldn't have to deal with all the DRECK that comes in here off the street to steal everything and disgrace this property with their filthy, ugly, dirty criminal habits that Mr. Robinson should DIE for because he does not have the sense, he does not have the gumption, he does not have the motherfucking ability to DO

HIS GODDAMN JOB, DO I MAKE MYSELF CLEAR, and I want him OUT OF HERE, that WORTHLESS snake—he's lower than a snake—and everyone else OUT of here who is too incompetent, or spineless or STUPID, and does not have the ability to perform their duties. IS THAT CLEAR?"

It goes like this for fifteen minutes. Prchal endures a verbal mugging, and each time she tries, calmly, to respond, he pounces again. His chest puffs, his fists are like rocks. My hands are on the table, ready to leverage a quick jump if necessary.

Prchal checks her watch at 7:20, stands quietly and leaves. A bit of the tension leaves with her, but not much. I sag at the picnic table, flattened by this display. She came to help, I tell Nathaniel, and yelling at her did neither of them any good. I tell him Stuart Robinson is a good man in my book, and that if Nathaniel expects to continue enjoying the privilege of an apartment and three meals a day, it's time to start treating them with more respect.

He nods, grudgingly, and I see a hint of regret in him as I leave. But before I'm halfway down the block, he's at war with himself again and howling. I can hear him all the way to my car. When I shut the door and turn the key, I get a symphony. The music on my car radio is so moving it almost brings a tear. Mozart, I guess. I sit for a few moments, overwhelmed by the beauty of the music and the contrasting ugliness of Skid Row. A drunk urinates against a building. A madwoman screams at her demons. A child of eight or ten, backpack slung over his shoulders, passes on the way to school. I kill the music and drive away.

26

My trip to New York has no agenda other than to know this one part of his life a little better. I want to walk the halls he walked as a twenty-year-old, pull his file and see his grades and teacher notations. I want to see the apartment building where he played Tchaikovsky's Serenade for Strings while looking out the window at the falling snow. There are so many things about him I'll never know. I don't know exactly what he hears and sees, nor can I begin to imagine. I don't know if he snapped because of the pressure of being black in a mostly white environment, a bad trip, the pressure at Juilliard, a chemical imbalance or some combination of all those things. I don't know if it's true that there's a fine line between genius and madness, or that musicians and other artists are more susceptible to breakdowns. When someone suggests that Nathaniel is an example of the latter, I tell them Skid Row is filled with housewives and plumbers and salesmen and truck drivers who all had breakdowns. Mental illness doesn't choose the most talented or the smartest or the richest or the poorest. It shows no mercy and often arrives like an unexpected storm, dropping an endless downpour on young dreams.

Nathaniel arrived in New York in the fall of 1970 after a year on scholarship at Ohio University, where he did very well but was restlessly determined to follow in Harry Barnoff's footsteps. He had nailed his Juilliard entry audition in late spring, calling Barnoff with the news, and he spent the summer studying with other Juilliard students at the Aspen Music Festival, where he was confronted for the first time with intense instruction and musicians who were at least as good as he. But if the air was thin in Aspen, oxygen masks should have been dropping from the ceiling at Juilliard. Nathaniel has told me about the butterflies he felt the first time he saw the gray slab that takes up an entire block at Lincoln Center on New York's Upper West Side.

Joseph Russo, Nathaniel's old friend and classmate, has agreed to escort me through the building, telling me that if you were good enough to be allowed past security and into the hallowed halls, you were assumed to be exceptional and expected to become extraordinary. That went for actors, dancers and singers as well as musicians. It was not uncommon for Nathaniel to retrieve his bass from the third-floor lockers and, while wrestling the bulky instrument to class, be forced to dodge a ballet dancer who was twirling through the hall, limbering up on the way to class. Actor Kevin Kline started at Juilliard the same year as Nathaniel. John Houseman was a teacher. Music filled the corridors and the air crackled with creative energy. It was an atmosphere some students found exhilarating and others found frightening, but there was more of the latter on the fourth floor, where dozens of tiny practice rooms, roughly the size of jail cells, line the halls. They could be torture chambers, Russo says, and the pain was never greater than when you heard another student playing better than you thought possible. No matter how good you were, someone was better, and across the street was Avery Fisher Hall, home of the New York Philharmonic and the best of the best. The math was pretty simple and the odds daunting. The vast majority of Juilliard's students would never set foot in Avery Fisher or any other concert hall without buying tickets. If he was going to be one of the fortunate few, Nathaniel, one of roughly twenty-five bass students at Juilliard the year he began, would have to do better than the bulk of his classmates, many of whom were from privileged backgrounds. He wasn't intimidated, but he was very much aware that he was the black son of a woman who ran a beauty parlor in Cleveland.

Room 315 was designed without air, windowless as a bomb shelter, and there isn't much in it besides a desk and a few chairs. It's the room where Nathaniel auditioned in spring and where he played again for his new teacher and mentor, Homer Mensch, who would decide which of three orchestras Nathaniel would be assigned to. Nathaniel was asked to play Camille Saint-Saëns's *Carnival of the Animals*, a staple in the string bass repertoire of orchestral solos. In Saint-Saëns's creation, the bass becomes an elephant, and Nathaniel did his confident best to coax a respectable pachyderm out of the plywood instrument his mother had bought him in Cleveland, used, for just over $100.

As Nathaniel played, Mensch, a former member of the New York Philharmonic, watched and heard everything. Right-hand bowing, left-hand slide-dance on the fingerboard, pitch, musicality. Mensch thought Nathaniel's music memory showed room for improvement and his ear was not quite fine-tuned enough yet, but he was struck by the young man's big, warm sound. Each note had feeling and expression, even when Nathaniel's pitch was slightly off, and his vibrato was striking, his left hand fluttering like a butterfly coming in for a soft landing. Mensch would have liked to see smoother and more technically adept bowing action, but the mechanical stuff was fixable over time. Sound was another matter altogether, and with some students, it couldn't be taught. You had it or you didn't.

Mensch decided Nathaniel was too good for the repertory orchestra but not ready to join the concert orchestra. He assigned him to the theater orchestra, and believed that with hard work, and lots of it, Nathaniel's potential was unlimited. "That Nathaniel can play," Mensch told Hal Slapin, a bass player who was in his second year at Juilliard when Nathaniel arrived. Not only did he have the talent, Mensch told Slapin, but the desire was equally evident. Nathaniel Ayers had not gone to Juilliard simply to get by.

Thirty-five years after he left, there's still a record of Nathaniel in the Juilliard vault, and it feels strange to hold his transcripts and recognize his handwriting. On his application, he lists his father's address as unknown. He lists his source of revenue as limited, with a small scholarship from a fund Harry Barnoff has managed to tap into in Cleveland. The file also contains his transcript and the half-sheet judgments of his jurors. They're like little report cards for the all-important auditions that were required for placement in orchestras and for year-end evaluation.

Nathaniel's first semester at Juilliard clearly did nothing to shake his confidence, but he discovered that his work had only just begun. He got an A-minus in his bass class with Mensch and an A in his theater orchestra class. But he drew a C in piano, and B's in ear training and music literature. In the second semester, he brought the literature grade up to a B-minus, but in ear training, he was down to a C-minus. At the end of his first year, another audition would determine how far he had come and whether he kept his scholarship. He played Saint-Saëns again, as he had when he first met Homer Mensch, along with Brahms and Koussevitzky, and his jury included three judges. There was Mensch; bass teacher David Walter, another legendary upright player; and Channing Robbins, an esteemed cellist.

Walter saw nothing not to like, and the grades he entered on the half-sheet scoring form were glowing.

Talent—A
Technique—A
Tone—A
Rhythm—A
Intonation—A
Remarks—Excellent in all respects. A+

Channing Robbins, who taught with Leonard Rose and was considered a technical master, particularly of bowing technique, was equally impressed.

Talent—Excellent.

Technique—Excellent.

Tone—Very full and vibrant.

Rhythm—Excellent.

Intonation—Excellent.

Memory—Used music.

Remarks—A very musical performance and a promising
    talent.

I feel as though I'm eavesdropping on the life of a young man in his prime, and this recorded history of Nathaniel's brief career fills me with pride and profound sadness. It's like looking at photographs taken moments before someone's unexpected death. I pause and sit back, gazing into the hallway at students as young and ambitious as he once was.

The most critical assessment came from Mensch, who knew Nathaniel best and was of the opinion that he was capable of playing better. He gave Nathaniel an Excellent for talent, but judged his tone, technique and rhythm to be merely good, and as for intonation, he wrote "generally good."

Overall, Nathaniel was handling the demands and the pressure with flair, even if, in Mensch's assessment, there was room for improvement. But nothing was out of the ordinary in that regard. Some students developed quickly, others took longer to hit their stride and many others dropped out and disappeared, never to be heard from again. In the case of Mensch, who saw so much potential in Nathaniel, he wanted to send the message that this was no time to begin coasting. Nathaniel's scholarship was extended, the jury decided he had passed muster to move up to

the concert orchestra the following semester and he was invited
to summer in Aspen again after a brief vacation in Cleveland. It
might have been a triumphant homecoming after a year in New
York City, at one of the world's elite music conservatories, but for
the fact that Nathaniel's family barely recognized him.

His clothes didn't match. His hair was messy. He was zealous,
jumpy, provocative. Jennifer remembers how uncomfortable he
made her with his nervous energy and awkward conversations. It
was obvious to everyone who knew him well that something was
different. From Aspen, he began calling Harry Barnoff and telling him the experience was overwhelming, and when he returned
to Juilliard for the fall 1971 semester, his grades began falling. He
got an incomplete in Music in Western Civilization, with C's in
everything else but orchestra class. When forced to sit for long
stretches through lectures and instruction, he was fidgety and
unsure of himself, his mind wandered and he felt claustrophobic.
He began hearing voices and looking over his shoulder to see who
was there, but it was like chasing shadows. Music was the only
thing that made sense. When asked to remove his string bass
from its case and make music, he was focused, reassured and inspired. Juilliard was constantly suffocating and reviving him.

"He was crazy," says Eugene Moye, a cellist who briefly roomed
with Nathaniel. Moye was considered a superstar, along with
classmate Yo-Yo Ma. But it was Moye's skin color—his father was
black and his mother white—that drew Nathaniel to him.

"He called me Gray Boy," says Moye. "Both of us were in
an extreme minority. He was a very angry black man, and very
anti-white."

Nathaniel took to drawing on the walls and ceiling of their

apartment, and did amazingly dead-on caricatures of teachers and classmates and scribbled musical references and racial epithets, turning their apartment into a mad tapestry of race-tinged, twenty-year-old angst. Nathaniel didn't stop until every square inch of surface was covered. He went ninety miles an hour all the time, filling the walls the way he filled time and space, ranting, raging, rapping about the great injustice done to the black man. "It wasn't a silly anger. It was a sort of informed anger and he was very adamant and very intelligent."

The only time Nathaniel calmed down was when he played music. If Moye's cello was nearby, he grabbed that instead of his own bass, amazing his roommate with his ability to hack out a decent sound on an instrument that required an entirely different understanding and sensitivity. Moye didn't care what Nathaniel played, as long as he stopped talking for a few minutes.

"He was fine when he was playing."

But there was more talking than playing. A month after moving in with Nathaniel, Moye packed up and left.

In the spring semester of his second year at Juilliard, Nathaniel got F's in music literature and visual arts. He got an incomplete in music in Western civilization and withdrew from ear training. His only A was in his concert orchestra class, where he advanced to the front line among bass players. In the third-floor orchestra practice hall, standing among peers and cradled in the embrace of Beethoven, Brahms and Haydn, he was steady, he was sane, he was at peace.

"Very sensitive musical playing," juror David Walter wrote at Nathaniel's year-end solo performance before the same three judges who had watched him play a year earlier. This time Nathaniel played the first three movements of the Bach Sonata No. 2. "Excellent bow control for expressive playing, possibly a larger dynamic spectrum on f side would be desirable."

Talent—A
Technique—A
Tone—A
Rhythm—A
Intonation—A
Memory—B+
Grade—A
Scholarship—Definitely.

Channing Robbins gave him the same glowing assessment as Walter, and Mensch, as before, was a little stingier, giving Nathaniel a B overall and recommending that his scholarship be renewed, despite his failing grades in other classes and his occasionally peculiar or aggressive behavior. If he could play this well, the teachers agreed, surely he could find his focus. No one on the jury seemed to realize that the promising young student from Cleveland was losing his mind.

In the Juilliard archives, the folder on Nathaniel contains no mention of what was happening to him. There is no indication, other than the F's and incompletes, that his greatest achievements as a musician were accompanied by the most devastating events of his life.

"Date of complete withdrawal, Oct. 6, 1972," says an entry in his file.

"Reason: Program too demanding at present."

One night, while visiting classmate Daniel Spurlock in his Upper East Side apartment, Nathaniel began asking Spurlock and his fiancée probing questions about their devout Christianity. Spurlock sensed that Nathaniel was trying to find a path to spiritual meaning for himself, so he happily obliged his fellow musician until Nathaniel's behavior took a strange, chilling turn. It began with a distant look in his eyes, and next thing Spurlock knew, Nathaniel began stripping off his clothes. His alarmed hosts called for help, and Nathaniel was taken to Bellevue Hospital's psychiatric emergency room. He was diagnosed with schizophrenia and calmed with heavy doses of Thorazine.

"I remember sitting in the cafeteria one day with several of the other guys and they told me that Nate had a severe breakdown," says classmate Hal Slapin, who never saw him again. Juilliard in the early 1970s "was not a place where students had much of an opportunity or were encouraged to bond. As one would expect, competition was stiff and Juilliard at that time was not at all a nurturing environment, especially for a student that was having any type of personal difficulty. I'm told that it is a very different place today, but back then it was survival of the fittest and there was absolutely no support for someone having personal problems. Students mostly went their separate ways simply because there was no alternative. Vietnam unrest was a pervasive part of the atmosphere, racial tensions were high, and students dropping out for all kinds of reasons was not at all an unusual situation. In retrospect, considering Nate's background and difficulties, Juilliard in the early seventies was probably the worst environment that someone as fragile as he could possibly have been in."

We were in my car once, listening to KUSC, when Nathaniel swooned over a piece the moment it began.

"Does this mean to you what it means to me?" he asked.

It was beautifully evocative, beginning with an expectant swell that suddenly pauses early in the first movement, like an infatuated suitor who stops just short of saying too much. The music was hope and longing, a poem to the idea of romance and the promise of love. My appreciation of music had grown immeasurably through Nathaniel. I felt it as much as I heard it, taking note of the mood changes and wondering at the themes. I marveled at the genius of creations so universal and lasting that they can survive death and war, the clamor of invention, the whims of style, the turn of centuries.

"What does it mean to you?" I asked.

"This takes me back," Nathaniel said. "I used to practice this at Juilliard. I remember standing in the window of my room at the Chalfont Hotel, playing this while watching the snow fall. There's the bass. Do you hear it? I can't believe that anyone could have something so brilliant in his head and have the ability to get it all down on paper, every note of it perfect."

"What is it?"

"It's Tchaikovsky's Serenade for Strings. Isn't it gorgeous? This takes me back. Does it take you back?"

Before leaving New York, I walk to the intersection of Seventieth Street and Amsterdam, where Nathaniel lived with Eugene Moye and with other classmates. I know he was in a corner unit on the tenth floor. I can see the window where he once practiced. I can hear the music as I stand on this busy, noisy corner, with cars and pedestrians streaming by and the subway thundering underground. One hundred and twenty-five years after Tchaikovsky created this music, Nathaniel has given it to me, making it new again. I understand the peace it brings him, a constant amid chaos in a language he speaks. I know the opening phrase and the way it humbles and inspires. I know the neat footwork in the second movement's waltz, and I see Nathaniel dancing to it with his bass, up in the window of the old hotel.

27

I still can't quite let go of the possibility that there will be a breakthrough, that he'll sign on for treatment or be one of those rare people whose illness dramatically subsides in middle age. But the visit to Juilliard is a reminder that for nearly two-thirds of his life, Nathaniel has been in a grip no one has been able to break. Not music teachers, not doctors, not his mother. He has survived in his own way and on his own terms, sustained for decades by music. Reluctantly, I begin to confront my own limits and try to accept that although I can help him, I'm not ever going to heal him. Dr. Ragins has had it right all along. The best thing I can do for Nathaniel is be his friend.

Nathaniel and I go to a Dodgers game and he cheers wildly for the hometown team, jumping out of his seat when the Dodgers rally against the Colorado Rockies. He announces to Section 29, while wearing a brand-new blue Dodgers cap, that he is thinking of abandoning the Cleveland Indians. We listen to classical KUSC on my car radio and it's like having a DJ on board, with Nathaniel narrating and patiently tutoring me.

Stuart Robinson talks Nathaniel into signing a contract saying he will abide by the rules, respect other clients and earn his keep by offering the wisdom of experience to newcomers. But Nathaniel's new sense of responsibility makes him even less tolerant of transgressions, so he muddles through the days alternating between model citizen and unruly agitator. There is one visitor who always lifts Nathaniel's spirits. He has fallen hard for Pam, the documentarian who sometimes takes him to the beach for a day and talks to him for hours in person and by phone. When Nathaniel ends up in the hospital with a bladder infection, she's the one he calls to pick him up and calm him down. He smiles at the mere mention of her name, but Robinson and I begin to worry that his infatuation has become an obsession, and that he'll end up with a broken heart. When Nathaniel hangs her photo in his room and begins calling her his fiancée, Robinson tells Pam it might be best if she didn't come around so much. Whether she wants to believe it or not, he tells her, she's giving Nathaniel the wrong impression.

To help Nathaniel get over it, I begin shopping for a new object of his affection. He says he used to play a flute but it was stolen when he got to Los Angeles, and he'd like to have another one. But as soon as I find one for sale, he changes his mind and says he'd rather have a trumpet. He played briefly as a teenager, he tells me, and when I suggest it might be time to choose a single instrument—preferably the violin or cello, since he's so invested in them—he sees no logic in that. Music is music, he says, and the more ways you can get at it, the better. And so I buy him a trumpet.

"It's not his best instrument," Robinson says with a pained expression after Nathaniel begins blowing his horn for hours every day in the Lamp courtyard, torturing both the crazy and the sane.

"It sounds like it's coming along," I say in defense. "He's got a bit of a Miles Davis sound, don't you think?"

Having a trumpet means needing sheet music. We drive to a store in Santa Monica and Nathaniel riffles through the stock for more than an hour, the proverbial kid in a candy store. He doesn't limit himself to trumpet music, declaring that he's never going to give up the cello or violin, so he needs this Dvořák, that Beethoven, this Bach and that Brahms. It costs me $662 to satisfy his needs, and it takes as long to check out as it took to drive to Santa Monica.

"Mr. Lopez," he says on the way back, "I'd like to see all of the columns you've written about me, if I could."

It's an odd request, given his usual lack of interest. By now I've written maybe a dozen columns about him and he's commented on one or two, as far as I can recall, telling me he doesn't really care to read about himself. When I've asked in the past if he has a problem with me writing about him, he has said he's flattered that I would consider him interesting or important enough. But I wonder if, for him, the columns are a sad reminder of what he once had, or if they read too much like a medical diagnosis he'd rather not hear.

I tell Nathaniel I was under the impression he didn't like

reading the columns about him. That's true, he says. But he'd like having them anyway.

And why doesn't he like to read them?

"It's more interesting to be out in the world," he says, "than to see it reflected in the mirror."

For all his troubles, Nathaniel has gone years without a worry common to the rest of us. He has no money, wants no money, needs no money. But, ordinarily, room and board aren't free. Nathaniel has been getting a free ride at Lamp in part because his story has generated donations to the agency. For other residents, a disability check helps pay the bills, but Nathaniel has been off the books for years and claims to have no interest in applying for Social Security. When I tell him a book or movie about his life can help cover his expenses, he insists he doesn't want the hassle of managing money he doesn't need, so I suggest we ask his sister, Jennifer, to handle his legal and business affairs. If she wouldn't mind, he says, it's fine with him. "Jennifer is a loving sister who's done all that I could ever ask of her."

I hire an attorney to draw up the papers, and Nathaniel meets with him at the Beethoven statue and plays violin for him. My friend is in a particularly good mood and showing off a bit. When the attorney asks Nathaniel if he indeed wants his sister to be granted authority over his financial affairs, Nathaniel says that sounds good to him, but he doesn't want to go to court himself. The attorney says he thinks that can be arranged.

Two weeks before Jennifer's visit, I drop by Lamp to hand

Nathaniel the paperwork. Although he doesn't have to appear in court, the law requires that he be notified of the conservatorship hearing.

"Do I have to go to court?" he asks when I hand him the manila envelope.

"No, but Jennifer does."

Nathaniel drops the envelope into his shopping cart and begins drumming on his cello case. He taps, taps, taps with drumsticks he's picked up somewhere, bobbing his head in rhythm. Everyone at Lamp is happier with his drumming than his bugling.

Two days later, I call Lamp to check on him. I'm on hold for several minutes before the receptionist comes back and says Nathaniel doesn't want to come to the phone.

"Does he know it's me?" I ask. He's never refused a call.

"Yes, I told him it's you."

"And he won't come to the phone?"

"That's what he said."

"This is a first."

"Maybe you can try back later."

When I call the next day, he again refuses to come to the phone. Now I'm getting nervous. With his sister due to arrive soon, I've tried to stay in close contact with Nathaniel and keep him in good spirits. He and Jennifer haven't seen each other in six years and I know how excited she is. On the third day, when he again refuses to take my call, I drive to Lamp and find him up on the landing at the top of the stairs like a sentry, blowing his horn.

"That sounds like it's coming along," I tell him.

He ignores me and it's clear something is wrong.

"I bet that would sound good in the tunnel," I say, mindful of the complaints from Lamp clients and employees. "You'd probably get a nice big echo."

He brings the trumpet down from his lips and finally acknowledges me.

"How've you been?" I ask. "I tried reaching you, but they said you wouldn't take the call."

He shrugs and pouts.

"Is something wrong?" I ask.

He takes two steps down the stairs, then a third, and stops. He's holding his trumpet like a weapon, shaking it at me from a distance of ten feet and threatening to come closer. His eyes burn, veins rise. His entire body is coiled, ready to strike.

I stay as calm as possible. If I relax, maybe it will cool the eruption.

"I'll tell you what's wrong," he says, his jaw tight. "I'm not going to any court and I'm not going to talk to any judge. What was that stuff in those papers about me having a schizophrenic mind?"

"That was just—"

"I'm not schizophrenic, and NOBODY, I said NOBODY, is going to take me to a hospital."

"You're not going to a hospital. That's not what this is about. And you're not going to court. Jennifer's going to take care of that."

"My little sister is NOT coming to Los Angeles."

"She's due in a few days, Nathaniel. She's very excited about seeing her big brother."

"Well, she is MY sister, and she is NOT coming here. And I

am not going to have any more of this Nathaniel, Nathaniel, Nathaniel. I'm Nathaniel and you're Mr. Lopez, and there is not going to be any more of that."

"Fine, and I'm sorry. From now on, you're Mr. Ayers."

"I don't want any of this nonsense because I don't need it. I don't need Lamp, with all these drug-addicted thieves and the incompetent people who work here and don't even do their own jobs. Animals are better than these people. Mr. Snyder, Disney Hall, the studio, you can keep all of that because I'm not having any part of it. Take the violins, the cellos, all of it. I'll go back to the violin I had in the beginning and go back to Cleveland. I don't have to stay in this STINKING town that I ABSOLUTELY MOTHERFUCKING HATE. I DESPISE LOS ANGELES. I DESPISE YOU!"

I feel sick, gutted, empty. He's shaking the trumpet as if nothing would please him more than to bash me with it. He's even closer to losing control than he was that day with Dr. Prchal, and I stand motionless, not frightened so much as broken. A Lamp employee steps into the courtyard to make sure he doesn't come after me.

"You can take the trumpet, I don't want it," he says, spitting the words at me. "I do NOT need ANY of this, and I do NOT need any probate court, no judge and no lawyer, and I will not have my sister Jennifer set foot in this city. EVER. DO YOU HEAR ME? EVER!!!"

The whole block hears him.

We're standing in the courtyard where I picked him up for Easter five months earlier, and he's turned on me in a way I never would have imagined. Has nothing mattered, the whole thing a waste of my time and his? This deranged twin has risen from Nathaniel's darkest depths, and Lamp employees hurry through the door again to see if I'm in danger. I motion to them that it's okay, that I think I'll get through this with my head still attached, but this is entirely new. He's never yelled at me, never threatened. I edge closer, thinking that when he looks me in the eye, he'll see more clearly the man who has spent a year and a half trying to help him. What he sees, instead, is betrayal. He thinks the court hearing is part of a plot to have him committed.

"I don't EVER, EVER, EVER want to see you back here again," he screams. "DO YOU HEAR ME?!!!"

I tell him he's got it wrong. Nobody's going to have him carted away against his will; we're only trying to help. But Nathaniel— Mr. Ayers—doesn't believe a word of it, and his self-control has short-circuited. His eyes boil and his screams are feral. The person he most trusted has lined up against him, or so he has convinced himself. I see the sharp, flat edge of the trumpet I bought him only a week earlier and imagine its imprint on my skull. I struggle for something to say or do, and all I can think of is the fact that music is his only medication, the only thing that soothes. I ask what pieces he's been working on, but he flicks my inept question away with contempt, as if only a moron would ask such a thing at this particular moment. He will destroy me, he promises, trumpet extended like a bludgeon.

"If I ever see your face again, it'll be the LAST TIME!" says the man who sat at my kitchen table and cooed over my daughter. Now he's calling me a motherfucker and with trembling hands orders me out of his life, guaranteeing that if I ever return, my guts will be spilled on the floor of this courtyard.

Do I call the police, run for my life or try to wait him out?

"I DON'T NEED ANY OF IT, DO YOU UNDER-STAND ME? And I don't EVER, EVER want to see your MOTHERFUCKING ASS here EVER AGAIN! Now Get OUT! GET OUT! GET THE FUCK OUT!"

I take a few steps back and stand at the door, listening to the echo. Another staffer checks to make sure he isn't going to try to beat me to death with the trumpet.

"If I EVER see you again, your blood will be in a PUDDLE on the floor. Now GET OUT, GET OUT. I DON'T EVER WANT TO SEE YOUR FACE AGAIN OR IT WILL BE THE END OF YOU!"

I can't take any more. I step outside the door and stand on the sidewalk. Stuart Robinson comes out and puts a hand on my shoulder.

"Are you okay?" he asks.

I can't speak. I look at him, unable to answer.

"It's all right," Robinson says. "He's having a bad day."

I've tried for months to help this man and I've accomplished nothing. It isn't his threat that bothers me. I don't take it all that seriously. What bothers me is seeing him like this. I'm his pal, and I know he appreciates everything I've done. Still, he can't stop himself. This is the way he torments Jennifer on the phone, calling her his best friend one time and psychotically cursing at her the next.

"He's so sick," I say to Robinson, barely getting the words out. "That's what bothers me the most, is seeing him so sick."

Robinson suggests I take a walk and come back another day.

"It's all right," he says. "It's all right."

28

I drive home and hug Caroline and Alison, feeling as though I've been away for months. Alison hears the details and her eyes fill. He'll come around, she says. He didn't mean any of it. I'm sure Nathaniel's mother told herself that a thousand times, and I'm sure she believed it. And yet each time had to be more difficult than the last. He was her son. Her only son.

For me, it's a low point that now seems as though it was inevitable, and there's a small measure of relief in knowing it's behind me. I mope around the house to echoes of Nathaniel's mad taunts, but their impact is blunted. I know I've done what I can. For the first time in my life, I've gone out of my way to help someone in need, and my conscience is clear. Yes, it all began with me looking to get nothing more out of the relationship than a column or two, but it became so much more. I experienced the simple joy of investing in someone's life, and the many frustrations have made the experience all the more rewarding and meaningful. I might not have always made the right choices in trying to help, but I came by each one honestly. I worked through the arguments for and against commitment. I wrestled with definitions of freedom and happiness, and wondered at times who was crazier—the man in the tunnel who paid no bills and played the music of the gods, or the wrung-out columnist who raced past him on the way home from sweaty deadlines to melt away the stress with a bottle of wine.

I read Caroline a story and put her to bed feeling blessed for my family's health, and I can't quite tell if this growing sense of contentedness is from exhaustion or the wine. Before falling asleep, I'm hit with another wave of sadness over the courtyard scene, but I feel absolved, too, as if his tirade was an act of mercy. I can't save him and I don't have to keep trying, nor do I need to be anything other than his friend. I close my eyes and let go, floating into deep sleep.

Two days after the courtyard meltdown, I haven't spoken to Nathaniel or checked on him with Stuart Robinson, but I'll have to drop by before much longer. His sister is due to arrive in a few days, despite his protests.

"I'm going for a bike ride," I tell Alison on Saturday morning. I'm planning to take the usual route along Riverside Drive and into Griffith Park, looping around the back of the Los Angeles Zoo. But after starting in that direction, I turn around and head for Sunset Boulevard. Sunset winds through Echo Park and into downtown, and I figure I'll go only as far as the Second Street tunnel. If he's there, fine. If not, I'll head back toward Silver Lake.

I cut south on Figueroa, curious about whether he still believes I've betrayed him and was setting him up, all along, to be committed. I'm also worried that if he ever calmed down and reflected on the things he said, he may be despondent. The suicide rate among people with schizophrenia is frighteningly high. In his rage, might he have done something to himself? Or has he packed up and moved out of the apartment, rejecting it as yet another trap in my efforts to have him committed?

I pick up speed as I glide down the gentle grade toward Second Street. This is the area where I looked for him that night, fearing he was in trouble when in fact he was spending his first evening in the apartment. My hunch is that he'll be in the tunnel now, to assert his control over his own destiny. I spent so many months trying to talk him off the street, arguing that it made more sense to live and to practice music indoors, he may be here as an act of rebellion.

I hit the intersection of Second Street and there he is. He's tied ten little U.S. flags to a speed limit sign and he's sitting on an office chair with the back missing, playing cello. He doesn't see me approach and then is startled to find me next to him.

"Oh," he says.

I realize I haven't even thought of what I might say.

"Mr. Ayers, I was just getting a little workout and thought I might find you here. Did you hear? The Dodgers pulled out another one. They're one game away from clinching a spot in the play-offs."

"They're going to be in the play-offs?"

"It looks pretty good."

"Do you think you could get tickets?" he asks.

I tell him I'll give it a shot.

"All right, Mr. Ayers, I've got to go."

"Mr. Lopez, you don't have to call me that."

"No, it's fine. I'm Mr. Lopez and you're Mr. Ayers. That's only fair."

"I don't want you to call me Mr. Ayers."

"Well, you're older than I am, you know. I should have been calling you that all along."

He gets up and stands before me, a different man than the one who threatened my life. His shoulders are rounded now, his body in a remorseful slump.

"I can't believe I said those things," he tells me.

"It's not a problem. We're friends and sometimes friends piss each other off, and that's just part of the deal. I didn't take any of it personally."

"I can't believe you'd still be my friend after that," he says.

The ride home is uphill, but I don't feel it. I pump hard around the Silver Lake reservoir three times, until the sweat is flying and the breeze feels cool on my face. I turn for home after the third lap and can't wait to tell Alison. I didn't need an apology from him. I only needed to know our friendship still meant something to him. He's okay, thankfully, and we'll go on from here.

29

Jennifer Ayers-Moore looks very much as her mother does in the jazz-age photo her brother keeps in his apartment, smooth-skinned and ageless, with pretty, clear eyes that hide neither her anticipation at seeing her brother nor the years of dread. We embrace in our first meeting after twenty months of phone calls and it feels as though we've known each other forever. Jennifer and her longtime close friend Kim, who has come along for moral support, have just arrived from Atlanta and are staying at a hotel six blocks from her brother's apartment. She and Kim are in the hotel restaurant for a quick bite, and they've taken the table farthest from the window that looks onto the street.

"I don't want him to come by and see us," Jennifer says. She remembers too well her brother's tirades, which terrified her and were like a dagger through her mother's heart. Jennifer is eager to get the legal business out of the way the next morning before going to see her brother. His blowup, she tells me, was undeniably related to the business with the court. He erupted manically many, many times when their mother forced the issue, calling the police or trying to hospitalize him.

Jennifer apologizes for his outburst and offers her thanks for my efforts, but I tell her there is no need. She knows the old Anthony, she tells me, the big brother who watched out for his sisters after their father left, who helped his youngest sibling with her homework and worked so hard to become a musician. She's glad that on the day I met him, I saw a glimmer of that person and was patient enough to get to know him in full.

It takes only minutes for a Los Angeles County Superior Court judge to declare that Jennifer can handle her big brother's affairs. We walk out of the courthouse and down the hill to the *L.A. Times* parking garage two blocks away, then drive toward Skid Row. Jennifer is rigid in the front seat. I've warned her about the neighborhood her brother calls home, because I know it will pain her. Not that she hasn't read about Skid Row in my columns, but in any description, words fall short.

"I've never seen anything like it," she says as we enter the homeless capital of the United States. Every street is a campsite and infirmary. I avoid the worst of it for her sake. I don't take her through the Nickel, the brokenhearted stretch of Fifth Street where the country's worst secrets are kept, a corridor of missing limbs and flattened hope, with dealers and thieves roaming like hungry wolves. But even at the edges of the epicenter, the streets are littered with trash and with lost souls, the majority of them

African-American. It's so striking I feel the need to explain it to Jennifer as best I can, as if apologizing for Los Angeles. But I don't know what to say except that the city remains largely divided economically and ethnically, and these were the ones who had no health insurance, no jobs that could cover the outrageous price of housing and no family to turn to when they became desperate or ill.

Jennifer sinks deeper into her own thoughts. I see traces of anger, compassion, guilt and helplessness. What could she or anyone in her family have done differently? What can they do now? This is where her big brother spends his days and nights, the musician, the brain, the handsome youngster the girls giggled over. He's landed out here with all these lost chances, and Jennifer is cut in half, anxious to see him but sick at knowing he is here.

"It's better than it was," I tell her as we approach Lamp, trying feebly to put a positive spin on a catastrophe. "Your brother had a lot to do with that, after all the attention this place got from City Hall. Of course, there's a long, long way to go."

I slow on the approach, trying to spot him in the courtyard through the fence.

"There he is," I announce.

Jennifer moves up in her seat. "Where?" she asks, straining to see.

"Right through there."

"Oh, yes," she shrieks, bounding out of the car. "That's him!"

Her brother spots us and rushes to the doorway, where he pauses as if considering whether he can believe his eyes. They hug in the corner of the courtyard, Jennifer in tears and her brother with a look of shock and relief. A half-dozen people loiter nearby, but brother and sister are oblivious, alone in each other's arms, a lifetime revisited in a single embrace. When they let go, he stands back and stares.

"You look just like our mother," he says, and then he turns to Kim. "She looks just like our mother," he assures her.

"We had some life," Mr. Ayers says to his little sister. "Didn't we?"

Mr. Ayers insists on giving his sister a tour of Lamp. She's so happy to see him that she temporarily tucks away her concerns about Skid Row and the asylum scene in the Lamp courtyard, where people are jawing at each other or settling scores with ghosts. Mr. Ayers insists on showing Jennifer his room, which I take as a good sign—pride of ownership—and a reminder of how far he's come from the days of tapping at rats with his Brahms and Beethoven sticks. By now, however, his room is a snapshot of his mind. It resembles a spider's lair, with police crime scene tape and cloth streamers dangling from the ceiling, and his doodles covering every square inch of wall like cobwebs. Beethoven's name is written a hundred times on the door of his closet, and one wall has been felt tip–penned into the set of the "Tonight Show Starring Johnny Carson," with "special guest Steve Lopez, *Los Angeles Times* staff writer." It's all too familiar to Jennifer, who has seen her brother torment their mother with his destruction of her home. All of her mother's pain is there in Jennifer's eyes, and all of her love, too.

Over the next few days, we visit the Beethoven statue, the Second Street tunnel and the slab of pavement at Los Angeles and Winston streets where her brother used to sleep. We all go to my house for dinner one night, where Caroline is excited about the visit and Mr. Ayers makes himself at home as he has before, serenading us on violin.

Jennifer has never been to Los Angeles, so the next day we drive along Rodeo Drive and under the swaying lollipop palms of Beverly Hills, a distant galaxy twelve miles from Skid Row. We take Sunset Boulevard through the forested glen known as Bel-Air and past the little outposts where hawkers sell maps of movie star homes. We tumble out of the hills under a deep blue sky and land on the shores of the Pacific. Mr. Ayers sets up his music stand in Palisades Park overlooking Santa Monica Bay and provides the soundtrack for a sun-drenched view that extends from Malibu to Palos Verdes, with Santa Catalina Island lightly sketched in the distance. He plays Saint-Saëns and Schubert, and Jennifer sits quietly and listens as she contemplates this strange universe. Santa Monica has its own teeming homeless population, a counterweight to Skid Row, and sad souls mill about with empty eyes, scabby blankets and this million-dollar view, even as an obvious drug trade goes on behind us near the public bathrooms.

Jennifer and I talked about trying to get her brother away from Skid Row at some point, maybe move him out here where the breeze moves in from across open water and the light often comes softly through the mist. But none of that can wash away the reality that just like on Skid Row, the help in Santa Monica is near the need, so the result is this little patch of hell in the middle of paradise. Jennifer and I would like to believe her brother can one day live on his own somewhere, take care of himself and do even more with music. To that end, I tell her the music studio could help, if it ever opens. If her brother slips into a routine there, and gets to where he can play and maybe even record with some of his friends from the orchestra, it might stabilize him to the point where he's open to treatment and maybe even medication. And if, and maybe, and possibly . . .

The weather is too nice and the people-watching too distracting to dwell on any of that now. Jennifer is with her big brother at long last in this crazy city their father moved to, breaking their young hearts. Strange, the way it has all worked out, with Jennifer taking over the financial responsibilities of a big brother who was always so wise and able. He plays now against a backdrop of sea and sky, a symphony under the trees, right here where impossible wealth meets hopeless suffering. Botoxed weight-watchers in designer sweats come jogging past drunken vets passed out on fields of green. Down the hill and across the cinnamon sands, the tide is up and the waves keep coming, a thunderous ancient rhythm.

30

Yo-Yo Ma is coming to town.

How do I know this?

Mr. Ayers is a walking billboard. He has scrawled the time and place on a white T-shirt and he's wearing it proudly. My name is up in lights, too, along with the LAPD.

"October 27, Disney Hall."

"Do you want to go?" I ask.

Dumb question.

Adam Crane of the L.A. Phil has a suggestion: Why not try to arrange for Mr. Ayers and Mr. Ma to meet after the concert?

Would Ma go for it? I ask.

Crane says that for such a superstar, Ma is extremely accessible. He sends an e-mail along to Ma's manager and suggests I do the same. In my message, I explain that although Mr. Ma might not remember, he and Mr. Ayers overlapped one year at Juilliard. I tell her that Mr. Ayers reveres his ex-classmate and is walking around downtown Los Angeles with Ma's name on his T-shirt. I send along a few of the columns, too, and I promptly get a response from Ma's manager.

Yes. Mr. Ma will gladly receive Mr. Ayers in his dressing room after the concert.

I'm as thrilled as Mr. Ayers will be, but worried about sharing the news with him. What if it doesn't work out for some reason? I don't want to get his hopes up only to see him get flattened.

On the day of the concert I visit Lamp to remind Mr. Ayers to get cleaned up and wear his finest, and I can't help myself. I tell him that I'm trying to arrange a meeting with Mr. Ma, but there are no guarantees. Mr. Ayers is okay with that. I also tell him I'll be picking him up a bit on the early side so we can make a stop on our way to Disney Hall. I have something very important to show him.

Mr. Ayers is wearing a Rite Aid polo shirt with a red and blue necktie. He has written "Steve Lopez" and "Mr. Ma" on the breast of the shirt, and over that he wears a black jacket of synthetic leather. His hair is parted in the middle and neatly combed, and he is carrying a briefcase full of sheet music as if on his way to work. Our first stop, I tell him, will be at Lamp Village.

"I'm going to show you the studio."

The idea is still fuzzy in his head, and it's time to clear things up. I don't know if it's another case of his being wary of committing to something he might not be able to hold on to, or if he has confused the music studio with his studio apartment.

"I don't need a studio," he says.

"Mr. Ayers, I've made arrangements for your piano to be delivered. They can't fit it in your apartment, so they're going to ship it to the music studio. The room isn't done yet, but I want to show you how it's coming along and what it's going to look like."

The short drive takes us past the Midnight Mission, where people by the dozens queue up for a cot or a patch of pavement for the night. Mr. Ayers would have to walk through this Calcutta each time he goes from his apartment to the studio, and I know he'll have plenty to say about it. I just hope the studio will be incentive enough to keep him coming through the gauntlet.

At the Village we stride down a long, shiny-clean hallway adorned with paintings by the residents. Near the end of the hall, three people sit in the glow of a big-screen TV. The studio is just past that, through a set of double doors.

"You see? They can get the piano through right here, but they'd never get it into your apartment."

Mr. Ayers peeks through the window of the locked door, taking in the dimensions. It's on the small side, maybe twelve feet square, but definitely serviceable. Casey Horan is having it soundproofed so Mr. Ayers can play to his heart's content without distracting anyone who doesn't care to be serenaded eight hours at a stretch.

"This is just temporary," I tell him. "They're remodeling the whole building, and a bigger studio will be part of the deal. But Casey didn't want you to have to wait any longer, so she's having this built to hold you over."

Mr. Ayers likes hearing that. Back in his apartment, neighbors sometimes complain about him playing at all hours, and now he'll have a private place. He stands there with his briefcase full of music, considering the possibilities.

"This is my studio?"

"There might be other musicians who use it from time to time, but you're going to be the artist in residence. Wouldn't it be nice to get up in the morning and have this to come to instead of arguing with the smokers in the courtyard? This is going to be a no-smoking studio. We should put your name on the door right here along with the No Smoking sign. Mr. Nathaniel Anthony Ayers, Artist in Residence."

He takes a step back, still sizing it up. I see in his eyes and his body language that he's chipping away at his instinct to resist anything new.

"This is really going to be something," he says.

Yes, he bickers with Lamp Community staff and other clients at times, but in better moments he offers respectful greetings and warm smiles, very much aware of a shared experience. This is his family now; his home. Mr. Ayers knows that, just as he knows this studio represents a second chance.

To Mr. Ayers, this is a chance to see what has come of the amazing talent he first witnessed thirty-five years ago, when they played briefly in the same orchestra.

"The youngster was off in his own universe," he says on our drive up the hill.

I ask Mr. Ayers if he ever spoke to Ma on campus or hung out with him. He says he can't recall for sure, but probably not. Ma trained under renowned cellist Leonard Rose, a full-time endeavor that left even less time for socializing than Mr. Ayers had. "The violinists and cellists are the quarterbacks," he says, "and this guy was on fire. I couldn't touch him, he was so hot. I was just back there with the bass section, happy to be in the orchestra at all."

We park and walk to the corner of First and Grand. The street is alive with men in jackets and women in gowns, an older crowd on its way to catch a star in the architectural gem that has become a cultural beacon. Mr. Crane is out of town on business, so Ben Hong, who knows Yo-Yo Ma fairly well, is there to greet us in the lobby and escort us to our seats. The same seats we always have in the orchestra section, just left of center.

"Are we still on to meet him after the concert?" I whisper to Hong.

He smiles.

"It's all set."

Mr. Ayers wonders if the whispering is about his meeting with Ma.

"It looks pretty good," I tell him.

Mr. Ayers chats with Hong about the all-Beethoven program and Ma's accompanist, pianist Emanuel Ax, another Juilliard grad. Hong tells him the two musicians know each other so well and have performed together so often, they don't need to rehearse. They'll play Twelve Variations on "Ein Mädchen oder Weibchen," Six Variations on an Original Theme in F Major, Sonata in G minor for Piano and Cello, Seven Variations on "Bei Männern, welche Liebe fühlen" and Sonata in D major for Piano and Cello.

Mr. Ayers says he would have preferred to see Ma backed by full orchestra on a Beethoven concerto, but it's a small concern, and it's gone the moment the musicians appear onstage.

"There he is," Mr. Ayers says, as if he were the PA announcer. "Mr. Yo-Yo Ma."

Having just two musicians onstage makes for a more personal and intimate connection for the audience. As Frank Gehry suggested in his vision of Disney Hall, it feels as if Ma and Ax are about to entertain in a very large living room. Mr. Ayers opens his briefcase when the concert begins and rummages for the sheet music he's brought. Hong, seated behind us, helps him find his place, and Mr. Ayers follows along. He looks up on occasion, whispering for me to get a good look at the fluidity of Ma's bowing, and he laughs heartily when Ma stirs the crowd with dramatic flourishes. At the completion of each piece, Nathaniel lets forth a hardy "Bravo!" As a valentine to the appreciative crowd, Ma and Ax encore with a selection from Mendelssohn's *Song Without Words*, then take their bows.

"Let's go," Hong says, and we weave our way through the crowd, down a spiral ramp, along a hallway and into a small dressing room. Mr. Ayers takes a look at himself in the mirror, training his hair into place and worrying about his appearance for such a big occasion. He wants Yo-Yo Ma to see a well-kept, self-respecting man.

"You look fine," I tell him.

Hong goes to check on Ma and returns to tell us it won't be long. Mr. Ayers is on his toes, bouncing, talking, checking the hair, tugging at his lapels. He calms himself by talking to Hong about the performance, calling it gorgeous. I stand back and watch in admiration. Ben Hong, Yo-Yo Ma, Emanuel Ax and Nathaniel Anthony Ayers have all passed through Juilliard on their way to something unknown, and though Mr. Ayers has taken a terrible fall, not one hour of practice has been lost to self-pity. Yes, he wishes he could take all the scattered notes and string them together. He gets frustrated by his lapses and sometimes even demoralized. He'd like to play an entire piece perfectly, all the way through, and he'd like to be good enough to play alongside great musicians. But even though all of that remains elusive, music still keeps his spirit intact, and he doesn't envy Ma, he admires him. Thirty-five years after they sat briefly in the same orchestra, their paths have intersected once more, a block from the tunnel where Mr. Ayers slept all those many nights next to his Little Walt Disney Concert Hall buggy.

Suddenly Ma appears, gliding into the room with an uncanny mix of star power and unpretentiousness. He's elegant in a black tux but exudes a casual, genial manner, and Mr. Ayers holds his breath and takes a nervous half-step back as Ma approaches, hand extended.

"You're an amazing player," Mr. Ayers says bashfully.

"Did you like it?" Ma asks. "I know you like Beethoven."

Mr. Ayers's answer includes a reference to "Mr. Ma."

"First of all, I'm Yo-Yo. Not Mr. Ma," the cellist says.

"I remember your hands from Juilliard," Mr. Ayers says, studying them as if trying to decode the magic.

It isn't clear if Ma remembers him from Juilliard, even though Mr. Ayers now cites several specific performances that have stuck with him over the years. Ma listens intently, then puts his arm around Mr. Ayers.

"I want to tell you what it means to meet you," he says, looking Mr. Ayers directly in the eye. "To meet somebody who really, really loves music. We're brothers."

Mr. Ayers doesn't know what to say. Ma tells him he'll be right back and returns seconds later with his cello.

Take it, he tells Mr. Ayers. Go ahead and play.

Mr. Ayers reluctantly reaches for the instrument and holds it awkwardly, the bow dangling from his hand. He looks at me with bewildered awe.

Go on, Ma tells him again. Give it a try.

"This is Yo-Yo Ma's cello," Mr. Ayers says as Ma excuses himself to greet other admirers.

"Go ahead," Hong encourages, and Mr. Ayers reluctantly fiddles just long enough to be able to say he played Yo-Yo Ma's cello.

It isn't easy to get Mr. Ayers to leave Disney Hall when the evening draws to a close. He talks with Hong about the life of an orchestra member, he lingers in the hall near the dressing rooms, strikes up a brief conversation with Emanuel Ax and stops before a gallery of L.A. Phil photos. Maybe it's harder for him than I realize.

"There's Mr. Hong," he says. "And there's Mr. Snyder."

It's getting late, and I have to drag him away from the gallery. I'd like to tell him he's had his own kind of success, and his achievements each day and every year are as commendable as those of the musicians he admires. But for a curse, his photo might be on this wall, too.

—⋙—

31

"*Yes, uh, Mr. Lopez,* this is Nathaniel Anthony Ayers calling. Hello to Jeffrey and Andrew Lopez, Caroline Lopez, Mrs. Lopez and of course yourself. I'm wondering if you're still planning to come to Lamp this morning. I recall you mentioning something about a surprise of some type. If you could get back to me, sir, I would appreciate that, and have a blessed day."

He leaves the message at my office, then calls me on my cell phone before I can get back to him. I'm driving to the new studio when he calls, along with Ben Hong, to drop off some presents and make sure everything is set.

"Yes," I tell him. "I got your message and I'm on my way with a special guest. Just give me ten minutes and we'll be there."

With Peter Snyder and Adam Crane out of town, Hong has asked if he can stand in for his colleagues and help Mr. Ayers celebrate the opening of his music studio. It's two days after Christmas, and I'm going to surprise Mr. Ayers with an upright string bass I bought from a jazz musician. The studio, with white walls and a blue carpet, smells of fresh paint. Hong says it reminds him of the little practice studios that lined the fourth floor of Juilliard. It's a place for a fresh start, with a box full of the sheet music I bought that day in Santa Monica. The big upright bass, which I delivered earlier, leans against the wall in one corner. And the donated Baldwin upright is in place against the wall, with a framed photo of Mr. Ayers and Yo-Yo Ma on top of it. Hong has brought gifts, as well. Cello strings and a Franz Schubert biography, which he sets on the Baldwin before we leave for San Julian Street to get Mr. Ayers.

"Ben Hong!"

Mr. Ayers can't wait for us to cross the street. He has been watching from the courtyard and comes toward us with all his gear, which includes the trumpet and a deflated punching bag he's been carrying around of late. He wears a plastic poncho even though a morning storm has already moved out, leaving behind a brilliant blue sky. My name is written on his cap along with "Donald Duck Concert Hall," sharing space with an embroidered likeness of Che Guevara. A pair of white-framed sunglasses are perched atop the bill as a fashion statement. We begin walking; Mr. Ayers begins talking.

"In Cleveland we had Severance Hall, Cleveland Institute of Music, Settlement Music School, Mr. Harry Barnoff on bass, Cleveland Municipal Stadium along the shores of Lake Erie, home of the Cleveland Browns, Mr. Jim Brown, Jacobs Field, The

Jake, Elliot Ness, Arsenio Hall and Mr. Henry Mancini, 'Moon River.' That's not a Beethoven city, though, like Los Angeles, which has the statue in Pershing Square, and I still cannot believe that Beethoven is there. A little bird told me he was there and I came upon him one day and I said, 'My God, Los Angeles must be his city.' He's not at Lincoln Center, where you have Alice Tully Hall, Avery Fisher Hall, the Juilliard School for the Performing Arts at, what is it, Sixty-fourth Street?"

We cross San Pedro and turn left on Crocker, with Mr. Ayers emptying his registry of every musician, athlete and music venue he can think of. It's a typical jumble, though maybe fueled a bit more than usual by nervousness and excitement. We've been talking about this day for months, and it has been made all the more special by the appearance of Hong, who has a natural, easy way with Mr. Ayers. Hong admires and even envies Mr. Ayers's relationship with music. For Hong, music is joy but it's also work, and there is no easy way to separate the one from the other.

Down the long hall we walk. I open the door and the three of us step inside.

"I can smell the paint," Mr. Ayers says, a bit stunned as he stands smiling in the center of the studio, eyes aglow. He points to the photo of himself with Yo-Yo Ma and giggles, then picks up the Schubert biography.

"He's one of my favorite composers," Hong says, and Mr. Ayers thanks him.

Like a kid on Christmas day, he doesn't seem to know what to play with first. He runs a few scales on the piano, then zips open the vinyl bag to get at the string bass.

"Merry Christmas," I tell him.

"This is huge," Mr. Ayers says, getting reacquainted after roughly thirty years of playing violin and cello.

He's right. The bass is so big it makes him look tiny, like the kid who fell in love with the instrument in Mr. Moon's middle-school music class.

"I've waited almost two years to hear this," I tell him.

At first, Mr. Ayers looks as if he's wrestling a bear. The fingering is entirely different than on cello and violin, Hong tells me. But a few minutes into it, the instrument seems more natural in Mr. Ayers's hands, and his left hand slides cleanly up and down the neck as his right hand plucks out a bluesy riff.

"He's got the groove back," Hong exclaims. "That's fantastic!"

Anna McGuirk, a neonatal nurse who donated the piano, arrives in time to help Mr. Ayers celebrate Christmas, New Year's and the opening of the studio that will serve as the new home for an instrument that has been in her family for forty years. By coincidence, she's the daughter of a carpenter from Cleveland, and after reading about Mr. Ayers, she thought he needed the piano more than she did. "An instrument has a soul," McGuirk says. "Instruments need to get played, and now mine will. That means everything in the world to me."

Mr. Ayers sets down his bass and plops himself back on the piano stool, warning that he isn't much of a player. But the way he runs the scales this time suggests he's been holding back on us. He picks up momentum as he limbers, and volume, too, and suddenly he is hunched over the keyboard and putting his shoulders into it, thunder-testing the walls of his new studio.

"What is that?" I ask Hong.

"Liszt," he says with a look of amazement. "A Liszt piano concerto."

"Can you play?" I ask, hoping Hong will take over on piano, with Mr. Ayers accompanying on bass.

"Not like that," Hong says.

When Hong begins playing Mr. Ayers's cello, the mood changes instantly. Nathaniel is at first awed and then crestfallen. Hong's earlier sense of Mr. Ayers's relationship with music wasn't quite right, and he realizes that now. His own skill is almost too much for Mr. Ayers to bear.

"Oh, my God," Mr. Ayers says. "I'll never be able to play like that."

True enough, he won't. But he'll be no less inspired by music than Hong or any other musician, and no one will play with more desire or love.

Shannon Murray and Patricia Lopez arrive to help christen the new studio. They were the ones who joined me at Second and Hill almost two years earlier. They were the ones who said they'd try to coax him in, warning me that this sort of thing can't be rushed. He'd do it in his own time.

Casey Horan is here now, too. The Lamp director is taking pictures, and Mr. Ayers thanks her for building the studio.

"Thank you for inspiring it," she says.

Mr. Hong had brought one more gift for Mr. Ayers that day—an invitation to see him at Disney Hall in a performance of Schubert's

Piano Trio in B-flat Major, with pianist Yefim Bronfman and violinist Bing Wang. Mr. Ayers is standing outside his apartment building when I arrive. For a man who doesn't wear a watch and has no clock in his room, he is reliably prompt, and our little pickup and shuttle routine is now a smooth operation. I pull up to the curb, he tosses his sheet music and a violin into the trunk, and we cruise over to First Street and up the hill to Disney Hall. Alison meets us in the lobby, along with Anna McGuirk, and Adam Crane leads us on the familiar path to our seats. Mr. Ayers tosses out a "bravo" when Ben Hong is introduced.

I sit through the concert, thinking back on two years that have been more exhausting and fulfilling than I could have imagined the day I first set eyes on Mr. Ayers. Maybe I'm now at a point of letting go, of recognizing the limitations imposed by so severe a disorder as schizophrenia. I have fought it from the beginning, wanting to believe things would be different in the case of Mr. Ayers, and even now I hold on to the hope that he might one day get past his fears, past the cyclical descents into paranoia and rage, and give a try to medication that could vastly improve his life. But I know it's not that simple, that there are no magic pills, and that thousands before him have gotten better only to chuck the meds and sink back again into the grips of incurable disease. I've learned to accept him as he is, to expect constant backsliding, to prepare for the possibility that he could be homeless again or worse, and to see hope in small steps.

I've never had a friend who lives in so spiritual a realm as Mr. Ayers, and I know that through his courage and humility and faith in the power of art—through his very ability to find happiness and purpose—he has awakened something in me. He is one of the reasons I thought seriously about leaving an industry in the throes of revolution, and he is the reason I've decided I'll never be happy doing anything other than telling stories. He has wiped away my professional malaise and shown me the dignity in being loyal to something you believe in, and it's not a stretch to say that this man I hoped to save has done as much for me as I have for him. I must confess that in the end, I gave up on both the violin and the cello, but returned to the guitar after an absence of twenty years, with Mr. Ayers encouraging me to get good fast so we could play a song or two together someday.

Mr. Ayers is received, after the concert, by his friend Mr. Hong, who confesses he was nervous onstage, knowing a fellow musician was up there in the audience, listening intently and watching his every move.

"It was amazing," Mr. Ayers assures Hong. "It must feel great to play so beautifully."

It's late, the concert behind us and another workday just hours away for me. But when I park in front of Mr. Ayers's apartment to drop him off, he makes no move for the door.

"Wait," he says as I begin to step out of the car. "Listen to this. This takes me back."

The piece begins as a beating, hopeful heart set to music.

"What is it?"

"Sibelius Number Two."

"Do you know it well?"

"Oh, my God, I love this piece. We played it over and over at Juilliard in orchestra practice."

"I don't hear the bass. Is there a full complement?"

"Right there," he says, pointing through the windshield as if an orchestra has assembled on the street. "Do you hear it? Bum-bum-bum-bum. Do you know how many times I played this?"

The Finnish composer's Second Symphony, more than a hundred years old, has swept up Mr. Ayers and carried him back to his youth. The music soars and plunges, whispers and roars. We're draped in moonlit shadows and for blocks around, people sleep on pavement, Sibelius rising over a murmur of troubled dreams.

"Do you know what Sibelius is saying here?" Mr. Ayers asks. "He's saying, 'I love this music.' Do you hear it? 'I love this music. I love this music.'"

He narrates the entire forty-minute symphony, fingering an imaginary bass at the start of the fourth movement, a suspenseful rhythm-driven march that creeps along hauntingly and then breaks into a full run, the entire orchestra joining the parade.

"I want to play," Mr. Ayers says. "I don't know if I could ever get back to the way it was, but I want to play. Do you think I could ever get back into an orchestra? I cannot believe how gorgeous that concert was at Disney Hall tonight. Did you see how perfect Mr. Hong was? It was absolutely flawless. How could he do that?"

Sibelius is drawing to a triumphant and dramatic close, much to the regret of Mr. Ayers.

"I don't want the concert to ever end."

ACKNOWLEDGMENTS

My sincere thanks to the many people who made this book possible, beginning with Mr. Ayers's sister, Jennifer Ayers-Moore. Jennifer's help with biographical information was invaluable, and her love and support of her brother have been an anchor in his life, particularly since the passing of their beloved mother, Floria Boone. Jennifer is as proud of her brother today as she has been at any time in his life, and knows better than anyone his humanity. Thanks as well to sister Del Lee and the Dicksons—Uncle Howard and Aunt Willa—for their help and hospitality in Cleveland.

I thank Harry Barnoff for both his insights and his undying support of Mr. Ayers. Thanks also to Gary Karr, another esteemed musician and former teacher of Mr. Ayers. I'd like to single out Joseph Russo, Mr. Ayers's former classmate at Juilliard, for his assistance with research, and for his continued efforts to reach out to his longtime friend and fellow musician.

Two members of the Los Angeles Philharmonic, cellists Peter Snyder and Ben Hong, have helped me understand and appreciate Nathaniel's gifts, but more important, they brought Mr. Ayers back into the brotherhood of musicians, beginning with Mr. Snyder's offer to become his teacher. No one from the Philharmonic has been more generous with his time or more interested in Mr. Ayers's welfare than publicist Adam Crane, who became one of Mr. Ayers's most trusted friends. My thanks to the L.A. Phil administration, as well, for being so accommodating.

I'm indebted to the entire staff at Lamp Community, which educated and inspired me. In particular, I'd like to thank Casey Horan, Stuart Robinson, Shannon Murray and Patricia Lopez. They expertly handled the task of allowing me access while doing their best to protect the privacy of their clients. Countless other Lamp employees also made me feel welcome, and so did the dozens of Lamp members who shared their time and thoughts. With every visit, I was more moved by their courage, dignity and strength.

Thanks also to Dr. Mark Ragins, who served as my on-call adviser, and whose book *A Road to Recovery* was an invaluable part of my ongoing education. And I can't thank Dr. Ragins without thanking the man who referred me to him—Richard Van Horn of the National Mental Health Association of Greater Los Angeles. Special thanks, as well, to the indomitable Stella March, StigmaBuster supreme, whose encouragement has been a constant from my very first column on Mr. Ayers. As March knows all too well, Mr. Ayers and millions of others have been defined by labels and socially ostracized because of them, making it all the more difficult to confront their condition and celebrate their lives.

My thanks to Dan Conaway for his belief in the story, and to my editor Peternelle Van Arsdale for her smart take on how to best tell it. I thank agent David Black for being David Black, a bolt of lightning and a good friend to boot. At the *Los Angeles Times,* I'm in the debt of editor Sue Horton, who helped craft the columns that led to the book, but who did much more than that. She was an active participant in the ongoing discussion on how to best help Mr. Ayers, sharing in my frustrations and my triumphs.

As she has done with my prior books, my wife, Alison, made great sacrifices to allow me the time, and she was, as usual, my best editor and most enthusiastic advocate. She supported this book, in part, out of love for Nathaniel, and shared my hope that the story could raise public awareness and help destigmatize mental illness.

I won't ever be able to adequately thank Mr. Ayers, who lives in his own world and was kind enough to let me in.

ABOUT THE AUTHOR

Steve Lopez is the author of three novels: *Third and Indiana*, *The Sunday Macaroni Club* and *In the Clear*. He is also the author of *Land of Giants*, a collection of columns from his days at the *Philadelphia Inquirer*. A journalist for more than three decades, Lopez has won numerous national awards for his work at several publications, including *Time* magazine and the *Los Angeles Times*, where he is currently a columnist. Lopez has two adult sons and lives with his wife and their daughter in Los Angeles.